T0165501

Memories of a Depression Baby
...Just Kidding Around

The Only Thing That Disappears Faster than a Summer Vacation Is Childhood

Sonja G. Farr

WESTBOW
PRESS
A DIVISION OF THOMAS NELSON

Copyright © 2011 Sonja G. Farr.

All rights reserved. No part of this book may be used or reproduced by any means, graphic, electronic, or mechanical, including photocopying, recording, taping or by any information storage retrieval system without the written permission of the publisher except in the case of brief quotations embodied in critical articles and reviews.

ISBN: 978-1-4497-2139-8 (sc)
Library of Congress Control Number: 2011911731

WestBow Press books may be ordered through booksellers or by contacting:

WestBow Press
A Division of Thomas Nelson
1663 Liberty Drive
Bloomington, IN 47403
www.westbowpress.com
1-(866) 928-1240

Because of the dynamic nature of the Internet, any web addresses or links contained in this book may have changed since publication and may no longer be valid. The views expressed in this work are solely those of the author and do not necessarily reflect the views of the publisher, and the publisher hereby disclaims any responsibility for them.

Any people depicted in stock imagery provided by Thinkstock are models, and such images are being used for illustrative purposes only.

Certain stock imagery © Thinkstock.

Printed in the United States of America

WestBow Press rev. date: 11/11/2011

Dedication

This book is lovingly dedicated to my mother, Corrie, and my daughter, Michelle, the two most loving mothers I have ever known. They have been the lights of my life and center of my world at different times.

But I can't leave out my daddy, Alvin, who knew everything that I needed to learn about life, and spent my childhood years and later trying to teach it to me.

Foreword

Why do I feel compelled to write this book? Primarily so that my grandchildren, Austin and Ashley, can read about their grandmother's childhood fun, antics and adventures and her time in history during the Great Depression of the 1930s and early 1940s in this country. I want them to see the world back then through the eyes of a kid who had fun and a great childhood filled with love in spite of what the adults were calling "hard times". I want them to understand that it is possible to enjoy life as it is and what you make of it, not just what can be bought to hold a child's attention and interest and entertain them. I want to write them a story that shows family value and the worth of being an individual, even without riches. And as my story ends, I want them to work at taking it a step further in their lives – to grow up with Christian principles, integrity, family values, honesty, empathy, sincerity, and kindness. I hope they can achieve all that while still maintaining a sense of humor and having fun "Just Kidding Around" while on their long journey into adulthood. Adulthood hasn't always been fun or easy, but being a child and having fun in spite of circumstances is what it's all about, and those memories can sometimes take the sting out of being an adult.

I hope others who read this account of a great childhood, which led to my own fun and principled adulthood, will try to travel this same road. We only get one shot at being a kid. I wish everyone could have as much fun as I did, and that they will try to see that every child they come into contact with has the same opportunity. It may make for a better world. What do you think? Read on, dear souls and find the answer.

By the way, if you remember things differently ....well, just write your own book. That is quite an experience, also

"Train up a child in the way he should go,
And when he is old he will not depart from it." Proverbs 22:6

Introduction

TO ALL THE KIDS WHO SURVIVED THE 1930's & 40's

After the trauma of being born, we were put to sleep on our tummies
in baby cribs covered with bright colored lead-based paints.

We had no childproof lids on medicine bottles, locks
on doors or cabinets and when we rode our bikes, we
had baseball caps, not helmets, on our heads.

As infants and children, we would ride in cars with
no car seats, no booster seats, no seat belts, no air
bags, bald tires, and sometimes no brakes.

Riding in the back of a pick-up truck on a
warm day was always a special treat.

We drank water from the garden hose and not from
a bottle. We shared one soft drink with friends, from
one bottle and no one actually died from this.

We ate cupcakes, white bread, real butter and bacon. We drank Kool-
Aid made with real white sugar, and we weren't overweight.......WHY?

Because we were always outside playing, that's why!

We would leave home in the morning and play all day, as
long as we were back when the streetlights came on.

No one was able to reach us all day, and we were
OKAY.

We spent hours building go-carts out of scraps and then rode them down the hill, only to find out we forgot the brakes. After running into bushes a few times, we learned to solve the problem.

We didn't have television, play stations, Nintendo's and X-boxes. There were no video games, no 150 channels on cable, no video movies or DVDs, no surround-sound or CDs, no cell phones, no personal computers, no Internet and no chat rooms.

We had friends and we went outside and found them!

We fell out of trees, got cut, broke bones and teeth and There were no lawsuits from these accidents.

We got spankings with wooden spoons, switches, ping -pong paddles, or just a bare hand and no one called child services to report abuse.

We were given BB guns for our 10th birthdays, made up games with sticks and tennis balls and, although we were told it would happen, we didn't put out very many eyes.

We rode bikes or walked to a friend's house and we knocked on the door or just walked in and talked to them. And we called their parents Mr. or Mrs. – not by their first names.

Our generation produced some of the best risk-takers, problem solvers and inventors ever. The past 70+ years have been an explosion of innovation and new ideas. We even sent men to the moon!

We had freedom, failure, success and responsibility, and we learned how to deal with it all. (Kind of makes you want to run through the house with scissors, doesn't it?)

IF YOU ARE ONE OF THEM, CONGRATULATIONS!!

My Arrival

I was born January 25, 1932 during the Great Depression era in this country. That tells you one reason I was an only child. My mama was Corrie Bemount Glosup and my daddy was Rufus Alvin Glosup. They were the most loving parents a child could have had. Times were hard, but love flowed freely in our home. My daddy was of German/Dutch heritage and my mama came from French descendants. I think that meant they came from people who never give up, and they displayed that trait and taught it to me.

It appears, at least from viewing photos, that I was a good looking baby with large blue eyes and a face that made my parents kiss it a lot. Our family was a very touching, hugging and kissing bunch. It was just an important part of our lives. Maybe the closeness of family was what helped to overcome the hard times everyone experienced during the Great Depression. This practice of family love and togetherness has continued throughout my life, so I guess it was a more important lesson to learn than the despair and depressed feeling so prevalent in the time I was born.

My mama and daddy both had jobs and seemed to be doing quite well before the Great Depression descended upon our country. They were buying a nice home in the Oak Cliff area of Dallas, Texas. Then they found out I was going to arrive in a few months. In those days women didn't work right up to the day before giving birth as is often done these days. So mama lost her job pretty quickly. To make matters worse, due to the bad economy, my daddy's salary was cut drastically. So there they were, left with less than half of the income they previously had, mama was pregnant, and they found that they could no longer maintain the payment on their house they so loved. They had to give it up and move to a small frame rent house. Sound familiar in these current days? Somehow history does seem to repeat itself if vigilance is not maintained throughout the land.

However, my parents and our close family survived and pulled up by our own bootstraps, managed to eventually own our own homes again.

During this whole process, I was growing up a fun loving kid that didn't seem to be aware of how poor we had all become - everyone around us seemed to be living in the same circumstances and we all just pulled together to help each other survive the adversity. Especially the kids. So read on to know how this kid managed to grow up a "Depression Baby, Just Kidding Around". It wasn't that hard, and it was a character builder and a spirit enhancer.

I will only write about the fun times I had as a child The world is too full already of sad stories, and it was back then, too. So let's just dwell on the fun and good memories of a great childhood in the midst of all that tragedy many years ago.

Some Baby Photos

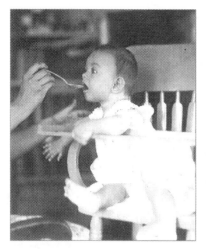

Wishing You
a very Merry Christmas and
the brightness of a Happy New Year

Wilton Street

Our House on Wilton St.

From the time I was a baby until I was in second grade, we lived in a small white frame house with a wide front porch. At least as I remember it, the porch was wide. It may have been just average and I was small, is why it seems wide now in my memory. The house had a living room, 2 bedrooms, one bathroom, a kitchen with the only small eating area in the house, and a screened back porch next to the kitchen. The porch had the screen door that led into the back yard and was separated from the kitchen by a wooden door. As you entered the front door, you came into the living room. To the right of the living room was my mama and daddy's bedroom. Adjoining it was the only bathroom in the house. (I will describe it in another chapter about an incident that occurred there.) My room was behind the living room. A long hall ran down the middle of the house from the front door, through the living room and ending in the kitchen. There was no central air conditioning or heating and no window units to cool the house. Those things were not being installed in houses at that time because they had not yet been discovered to be items that could be built into a small home like ours. Back then we had fans to cool us and gas or electric heaters to warm us – or a seat next to the kitchen stove occasionally.

One space in the house that was very unusual was the pantry to one side of the kitchen. It was a walk-in pantry and you entered it through a wooden door that looked like any of the other doors going into a room in the house, but when you entered the pantry you were in a long narrow "room" with a small high window at the end. As I recall, it seemed to be approximately 6 or 7 feet long and about 6 feet wide. That is, there was about four feet of walking space from side to side, and each side of the little room had shelves from floor to ceiling. Since there was not much cabinet space in that small kitchen, that is where my mama stored her canned vegetables, boxed foods, baking goods, cleaning supplies, some pots and pans, as well as her waffle iron and other household and kitchen items. Our vaporizer and cough syrup were also stored there. Why not store cough syrup in the bathroom medicine cabinet? I'll tell you why.

My daddy was a deacon in the Baptist church. The rule was no drinking of alcohol and neither he nor my mama ever drank. But the little canning-type pint jar full of clear bronze colored liquid, with rock candy in the bottom, was my cough syrup – not anyone's whiskey – even though that is what it really was. It wasn't a doctor's prescription, just an old family recipe that filtered down through the years to quiet a kid's bedtime cough. It was the magic elixir, given one small teaspoon at a time, that would almost immediately quiet my nighttime cough and help me relax and fall asleep peacefully. It was sort of sweet, due to the rock candy, I am sure, but it was hot and burned a bit when it hit the back of the throat, so swallowing it quickly seemed to be the best thing to do!. It didn't taste bad – just strong enough to sort of take away your breath for a second. Of course it had to be kept on the highest shelf in the back of the pantry, hidden from view behind a box of something. It wasn't put there just to keep it away from me, because I could scramble up those shelves at an early age to explore the wonders of the pantry. Climbing was my specialty, not getting into that hot rock candy cough syrup. It was kept there to be out of sight. I didn't find out until years later what it was and why it must be hidden from view. However, no matter what it was made of, that spoonful of liquid given for a cough at night, and which burned going down, was enough to put an end to my cough and made the recipient of that home remedy sleep for the remainder of the night! These days I notice that the cough syrup bottles on shelves in drug stores have a comment on the labels that the product "contains no alcohol". Apparently the cough syrup manufacturers are not aware that the magic elixir – or whiskey – or alcohol – could quiet a cough, comfort the throat, and help a little kid relax and sleep soundly. Some people still have this magic elixir in their homes, out of sight in their pantry, but not to quiet a nighttime cough!

In summer when it became hot at night, I sometimes slept on the bed on our screened back porch. It was still a pretty warm place to sleep but there was a floor fan that was plugged into an electrical outlet in the kitchen and placed in the doorway to blow over my little bed out there. My mama and daddy also had a similar fan, and all the windows were kept open at night when it was very warm weather. No, we didn't seem to worry about anyone climbing through our open windows. Nobody ever seemed to do that back then. Folks even left their keys in the car sometimes. That sure wouldn't work today! Wonder where all the thieves popped up from who break into homes in better economic times than during the depression years. Go figure. There must have been more of a stick together and survive attitude during the Great Depression. I was never scared. I was too busy just kidding around most of the time to be bothered by other stuff.

And let me say right here that it was just as hot in summer back then and just as cold in winter, but we managed to survive with our primitive cooling and warming appliances anyway. However, I wouldn't trade my present day cooling/heating system for those used when I was a kid. Maybe one reason we frequented the movies and large department stores in the summer was to take advantage of their cool interiors.

One of my earliest recollections of Wilton St. was when I went clopping across the driveway of our little rented house wearing my daddy's brown leather slide-in house shoes, headed next door to my aunt's house. I couldn't have been more than two years old, but I can vividly remember doing that. For some reason, never explained to me or questioned by me, my aunt and her family, my grandmother, my mama and daddy and I all lived on the same block only a few houses away from each other. I don't think that was the norm in those days, but it suited us all very well. We were a very close family, and having my mama's sister and mother a few steps away helped to cement that small family unit. My daddy's family had all scattered in different directions and different states, so he was surrounded by females of mama's family.

We all lived in small white frame houses that looked entirely different from each other. All three had frame detached garages out back. My daddy built a small "stage" and attached it to the back of our garage later for the purpose of neighborhood shows put on by me and my playmates. As I grew I loved to dance and sing and play make-believe, and that little stage was a perfect spot to do so.

We had a fairly large backyard, but no fence. My aunt's house had one of those rather short red wooden picket fences with sharp tops on the pickets. It was held together with heavy wire. Sounds pretty primitive today! Her fence was to keep her chickens from running around the neighborhood. My grandmother also had a similar fence and chickens all over her backyard. Since we had no fence and no funds to build one, my mama and daddy had no chickens. We did, however, have some great fried chicken meals, courtesy of my aunt and grandmother. Meat at the meat market was expensive in those depression days and chicken was a nice, less expensive alternative, especially if they were homegrown chickens. But I hated those chickens on the run in my aunt's backyard. I will tell you why later.

We lived in that little rented abode until I entered second grade. Read on and I will tell you about the good times we had there.

Checking out the rose bush. Watch out for those thorns!
Kids have to learn the hard way.

Toddler Transportation
Check out the "high fashion" sun suit!
I can't believe I had shoes on.

The Sling Shot

y daddy told me a story about something that happened when we lived on Wilton Street shortly after I was born. It involved a neighbor's dog next door, and I want to share it here for posterity because it is so funny. My mama said it was true, and my daddy never lied, so I have to believe it actually happened.

The people living next door to us (on the opposite side from where my aunt lived next door to us) had a dog. It was a large dog and they had a tall wooden fence to keep the dog in their yard. That dog insisted on barking constantly when those folks were not at home. Apparently this incessant barking would wake me when I was a new baby trying to sleep. My daddy got really tired of hearing that dog one late afternoon, so he went for his weapon. No, he didn't plan to shoot the dog. He had a plan to stop the noise, however. My daddy was a crack shot with a forked apparatus with a rubber strip attached to either side and a handle below the forked wooden top. I think you would call this a form of slingshot, except that it wasn't slung. You put a small pellet or maybe a rock into the rubber strip while holding the handle with your other hand and pulled back on the strip and when it was sufficiently tight, you let go of it and it propelled the chosen missile toward the target. My daddy could take a small pellet and insert it in this apparatus, draw it back, aim it, release it, and strike his target with deadly accuracy, even from several yards away. This was achieved after many years of practice, he told me later.

One evening just at dusk the neighbors next door left home for the evening. As soon as they were out of sight, the dog began barking incessantly. Or course that time of day is when small babies usually are sleeping. I must have been doing just that, because my daddy decided at that point to take matters into his own hands. He had prepared ahead of time apparently, since he had taken a large knot out of the side of our wooden detached garage. It left quite a large hole in the garage wall. This faced toward the back yard of the house next door where the barking dog was carrying on again. Of course my daddy didn't want everyone to see what he was about to do, so he quietly slipped outside and into the garage where he had previously left his shooting tool and pellets. He inserted the pellet into the strip and peered through the hole while holding the shooter, fully cocked, in front of his line of sight, aimed toward the neighbor's board fence. The missile hit its target with such force that that it made the dog stop barking and then the animal jumped up on top of the garbage can which was sitting in a rack at the corner of the fence below the overhanging roof of the house. My daddy fired off another round and hit the fence again next to where the dog was sitting on top of the can. This time the dog jumped from the top of the can to the top of the wooden frame that held the can. He still wasn't barking. This was right next to the overhanging roof, but not under it, at about the same level as the sloping roof. The dog began yelping again, so my daddy drew back and fired another pellet at the fence. It hit with great force again and when it hit, the dog jumped from the garbage can rack up onto the house's sloping roof! The barking stopped and the dog made his way slowly up to the peak of that part of the roof and just sat there. Things got really quiet after that, so my daddy quickly exited the garage and went back into our house. He told me that when that neighbor family returned it took them the rest of the evening to get that dog down from the roof!

After that, all my daddy had to do when the dog began his barking was to go back to the garage, remove the knot in the side of the garage and fire another round through that hole and smack that fence with a pellet. That hound was so scared by his rooftop episode that he would crawl into the corner under the garbage can holding frame and stay there quietly. Smart dog! I have never heard of anyone else doing this, but whatever works, I guess. The best part of the story is that the neighbor never did figure out how or why that dog ended up on their roof!

Speaking of dogs, I must remark that we also had a dog…a big German Shepherd who roamed around our backyard on a long tether attached to the clothesline pole. Oh, you don't know what a clothes line is? There were no dryers – or even indoor washing machines – in those days, so two pipes with smaller pipes welded on top to form a "T" were stuck in concrete sunk into the ground about 20 feet apart. Then a couple of heavy wires were attached and strung between them at either end of the "T".

Wet clothing, towels, sheets, etc. were then hung with clothespins on the wires to blow in the breeze and dry. (Don't tell me you don't know what clothespins are!) These poles were a good place to anchor a dog when there was no backyard fence.

Now, back to our dog. There was no leash law in those days and our dog would probably have just wandered around our backyard without being tethered, but my parents were worried that he might wander off and get lost. Actually, his "job" was to guard our "meter house". Don't know what a meter house is either? Well, let me educate you. A meter house was a narrow wooden box about five feet tall, which was attached to the back of our house to cover the electric meter. So why guard it? In those days, folks stored their empty bottles in those little boxes next to the meter until time to sell them for a few cents. Since money was so precious and so many men out of work, if you didn't guard those bottles, someone else would come at night and steal them for the few cents they brought. Even our milk came in glass bottles in those days, so it was not hard to collect several of them in a month's time. One evening our dog began growling and my daddy went to look out of the back window to see why he was growling. He saw a man trying to get into the meter house. He was going to steal our bottles. My daddy dashed out the back door and confronted him and the man ran around him and toward the front of the house to make his getaway. My daddy ran to the garage and grabbed his slingshot and pellets and began chasing the man down the sidewalk. The guy was apparently pretty slow and my daddy wasn't, so when he got closer to him he took aim at the guy's rear end and fired a pellet. Needless to say, that potential thief's speed increased! My daddy thought the guy probably got the message, so he returned home. We never had guns in our house. Didn't need them. My daddy armed with his slingshot worked quite nicely, thank you!

Tornado

I was too young to remember the tornado that almost took our house and actually did take away the house across the street, resulting in there being a vacant lot there during my early childhood.

I must have been less than a year old, since (as I recall) my parents said that the tornado hit in 1932. With the absence of TV, which had not been invented and available for family use yet, folks didn't have a warning about these heavy storms and tornados. There were no warning sirens sprinkled throughout the cities either. You just had to "feel the weather", as my grandmother used to say, or during certain months keep a watchful eye on the clouds. Even then, sometimes it was impossible to get out of the way of a tornado.

During this tornado in 1932, a path of widespread destruction was caused across a portion of Oak Cliff, the Dallas suburb where we lived. My daddy and mama heard that tornado coming. They quickly pulled the mattress off of their bed and it into the hallway and put all three of us under it to protect us from any falling debris. Good thing they did! The tornado wind damaged the roof of our house and the hail, which they said was the size of golf balls, broke through the window screens and glass and rolled across the floor into the living room of our house. Rain came in and soaked the floors, creating a large mopping and cleaning job for my parents.

When the storm died down and my daddy and mama looked out the front door to get a view of other damage to the neighborhood, the house across the street was mostly gone! Debris was all over the place, but the house was mostly just swept away in the wind. I cannot remember what my daddy said happened to the people who lived there, I hope they were not at home, I also cannot remember ever having seen them. It was just a vacant lot across the street for years as I grew up, but undoubtedly there was a story. I wish I knew. I think about that incident every time my granddaughter watches our video of "The Wizard of Oz".

My Daddy's and Mama's Occupations

As I told you previously, my mama worked in an office before I was born. Then my mama discovered she was pregnant with me! She had miscarried earlier in their marriage, so they had waited for several years before trying to have children. They were in their 30s by that time. It wasn't the best time for them to have a child, with all their other problems, but lucky for me, they did.

My mama never returned to a job outside our home after I was born. She was content to be a homemaker, and at that task she was super! Home was a haven. My daddy, on the other hand, was very conscientious about being the family breadwinner. It sure worked perfectly for us.

My daddy had been involved in weight lifting and body building activities for several years. He attended many weight lifting meets popular in the 1920s and 1930s, as a lifter and also as a judge. He was a pro at it and had the body to prove it. He was a perfect example of a lean, muscular and fit body. His goal seemed to be to improve the body and health of every man with whom he came into contact. My daddy was a good-looking guy with black wavy hair, sky blue eyes and beautifully tanned skin. He was always so crisp and starched and polished looking that other guys must have wanted to look that good. My mama had brown eyes so dark that it was hard to even see the pupils of her eyes. She also had dark wavy hair. She was a very short lady who had to stretch to make 5 feet and 1 inch in height. She loved being a homemaker and could not have cared less if she worked outside our home a day in her life. Her cooking skills were outstanding! She could make just about anything "from scratch", and even made veggies delicious enough for a kid to enjoy. What a beautiful pair those two made. And what wonderful parenting skills they both had. Both of them always urged me on to do all I could to achieve my goals. Today's world needs more parents like them.

Now, back to my daddy's occupation. After struggling along for a while with a new baby, on a half salary in a small rented house, another career possibility suddenly became available to my daddy. It was something he had wanted to do for a long time. I was a toddler at the time that the position of Health Club Director of the YMCA in Dallas became available. My daddy applied for it and was successful in landing the perfect job for himself. At that time, probably nobody at the "Y" really realized how devoted my daddy would be to his job, or how he would help to expand the "Y" programs, or even how many years he would devote to the YMCA. He was occasionally asked to work with other YMCA locations to assist them in building their Health Club programs. He never had another job while I was a child. The success that he accomplished there was his life's ambition.

When he took his new position with the "Y", one activity for which he was responsible was the training of the men who did the massaging of the Health Club members. He was glad to have this opportunity, since he had previously studied some of these procedures and as he taught his new students, he incorporated many of his own forms of massage therapy into the program. My mama and I also benefited over the years from his expertise in that area by frequently enjoying a massage at home. They were wonderful and really loosened up your muscles and relaxed your body before bedtime. My favorite was the rippling back massaging and also the pulsing arm massages which ended in finger pulling and limbering. (Don't knock it if you haven't tried it) Many times as an older adult, I have wished for my daddy's relaxing massages on my neck, back and arms. Those Health Club members at the "Y" must have enjoyed them, also, because many of the men began coming back several days a week for massages by my daddy's students. Of course, his specialty was weight lifting and exercise for body-building, so those massages were a great way to finish the workout programs he put the members through.

My daddy's hobby was photography, and he quickly incorporated that into improving the health and physical development (or "correction", as he called it) of men who took advantage of his programs. Through photography those men could see the progress of their body-building, sculpting and "correction". When overweight or out of shape men came to the "Y" to exercise, lose weight and shape up, my daddy would sit down with them to create an individualized plan for their goals. His method after that consultation was to have them undress, stand behind a white screen which was back-lighted, and photograph them facing forward, from the side and from the back, producing silhouettes of their bodies from all angles. Most of those men didn't even realize just how out of shape they really were until they viewed their silhouettes. Then they were ready to work with my daddy to do something about improvements. The "Y" had a darkroom downstairs where my daddy developed and printed those belly fat revealing photos. He took those "before" and "after" photos periodically to show the men their progress and to spur them on to reach their goal of a better physical condition and appearance. Most of the men could not believe how much better they were beginning to look and feel. He kept those photos locked in strictly confidential individual files and reviewed them only with the member in the photo. Even though they would have been good for a laugh in some instances, he wouldn't even show them to my mama or me, even though we didn't know any of the men. He was a stickler for privacy along with good health! In addition to the physical help my daddy offered these men, he also gave them a list of foods that would be a better diet for them on which to concentrate while they were re-building their bodies. One of his favorite quotations was "you are what you eat, as well as how you exercise". As soon as my daddy was satisfied with the individual results of a man's body improving work, he would take the final set of photos. Of course, after they had completed his program, all these "before" and "after" photos were given to the men to encourage them to keep their bodies in good shape. Most of them continued to work out with my daddy on a regular basis, though not in as stringent a program, to maintain their new fit appearance.

The transformation of the men who stayed with the program was amazing. There was nothing like seeing their progress in "black and white", as my daddy presented them their set of photos. His reputation grew and he was widely sought for his help and encouragement by many men in the area. It also increased the number of men coming to the "Y" for this service in the Health Club. Since there were no fitness clubs in the area in those days, that trip to the "Y" was it for many men, and my daddy was the man to work with for bodybuilding success.

In addition to his Health Club success at the YMCA, my daddy also took on another activity for the "Y". This involved working one evening per week to teach a course in "mind building" rather then body building. He took the responsibility of teaching the Dale Carnegie course "How To Win Friends and Influence People". And what better person to teach that! He practiced what he taught before he even read the book. He never considered it a chore. They could not have chosen a better person to teach that course. He was a natural. My daddy was probably one of the most charismatic people I ever knew. It was like people were literally drawn to him. I learned a lot from him, but would never be able to match his charisma or magnetism. Few people could. I was just a little kid, but I knew.

It was so great to have a mama who laughed a lot and always seemed happy, and who catered to my daddy's and my every whim and need with loving hands, and to have a daddy who drew so many interesting people to him and to our family. Childhood was wonderful with parents like that – even in hard times during a depression – no kidding!

My daddy, the weight lifter!

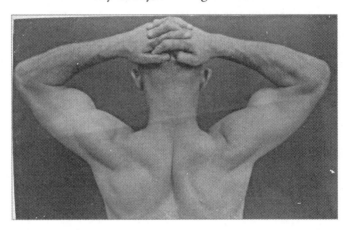

A real muscle man!

Dressing Up for the Milkman

When I was a small child on Wilton St. our milk was delivered by a milkman, right to the back door and into the refrigerator – the one with the round thingy on top. If you didn't sell your milk bottles along with your other glass bottles, you set them (cleaned of course) out on the front steps, and the milkman delivered however many you needed to replace the empties. Our milk came in quart bottles with paper covers that were sort of "pleated" and clamped down on the bottle top. Much different from today's plastic bottles with plastic tops that must either be pried off or unscrewed only to reveal another paper that must be removed also. Surely this is much more sanitary today, even though more difficult to actually get to the milk.

Even though I was about age 3, I can vividly remember this incident that happened one day when I was playing inside our house and amusing myself while my mama did some kitchen cleaning. I raided her lingerie drawer and found her panties. I pondered a while as to how to amuse myself with them and decided to slip into a pair. Since they were much too large for me, of course, I pulled them over my clothes and all the way up to my neck, where I clipped them in place over each shoulder with a couple of clothes pins. I then searched for something to fashion a hat or some kind of headwear. I rummaged around for a while until I came upon my mama's box of sanitary napkins. At this point, my mama should have been alerted to check on me since I was so quietly playing, but she was too busy, I guess. Her mistake! I removed one of the napkins from the box and was delighted to find that it would fit on top of my head, and that the long tabs at either end would tie under my chin. (Let me explain here that in those days the napkins were attached by the long tabs front and back to a narrow elastic belt worn around the waist under panties.) Of course at that age I had no idea what the sanitary napkins were used for. To me, they were just sort of fluffed hat material with chin ties. I looked so good with my new attire, I thought, that I went in search of some matching footwear. I found a pair of my mama's white spool heel shoes in the closet and decided they would match my new ensemble. My mama had very small feet, size four shoes, so they didn't flop too much on me. Just enough to make that desired clopping, clicking noise.

As I was admiring myself and my new clothing line in the mirror, I heard the milkman arriving at the back door with his milk delivery. I immediately ran to the kitchen to show off my new outfit. When he came into the kitchen, I told him those were my new "rompers" and bonnet. My mama just stood there open-mouthed and turning red, unable to say a word! She just froze! The milkman just about lost it right there. I thought he just didn't like my first attempt at fashion designing and I sort of got my feelings hurt. He finally gained his composure and complimented me on my selection. He then poked the milk into the refrigerator and left quickly, not looking at my mama, while she tried to gain her own composure. I left the kitchen and happily continued my dress-up game. Funny what you can vividly remember at an early age. Probably because it was a bit traumatic. I am sure my mama and the milkman never forgot that episode also. It probably made a good story for him to tell his other customers, too.

Imaginary Friends

I have discovered, after talking with old friends, that I was not the only child who had an "imaginary friend." I haven't looked into the psychological reason for that early childhood practice, but I would imagine that it was because of the lack of a sibling. In other words, sort of an "only child syndrome" type of action on the part of a small child with nothing to do sometimes and nobody to do it with. Now there is a subject for all the child psychologists reading this to tackle, if they haven't already done so. When I asked my daughter if she had ever had an imaginary playmate/friend, since I did not remember her having one, she just looked at me strangely and said, "Well….no" Apparently it sounded pretty goofy to her, and she actually did have a brother.

In my circle of friends who had an imaginary playmate, I have found that I was the only kid who actually gave him a name. His name was "Dockie". I have no idea why I gave him that name. It doesn't apply even remotely to anyone I ever knew. Just something that oozed out of a little kid's mind, I guess. I still remember him by name, but not visually in my mind. He had no visible body to me. We just played at something and I talked to him. In fact, I don't remember his ever talking back. Maybe there is something deeper to that, also.

When I was very small and living on Wilton St. I had only little boys to play with. Perhaps that is why I thought my imaginary friend was a boy and played with him when the other little boys were not available. I baked cookies with Dockie on my little toy electric stove, I brushed my teeth with him, I played paper dolls with him, and whenever I left the house going somewhere with my parents, I always stashed him behind the door leading from my mamma's and daddy's bedroom into the bathroom and told him to stay there until I came back for him. I can remember making a big production of putting him there and telling him "you stay right there, Dockie, until I get back home". They always had to wait for me to do that if I was playing with him.

It's a wonder my parents didn't have my head examined! This lasted only about a few months they said, and I guess I just outgrew the need for Dockie to play indoors with alone. My theory is the "only child" syndrome need for a playmate that could be made to appear and disappear at will sometimes. During the Great Depression there were a lot of "only children" because folks just could not afford more mouths to feed. At a luncheon not long ago, I discovered that all but one of the people sitting at my table was an only child born about the same time I was born. I didn't bring up the imaginary friend subject at that lunch table, however. They might have thought I was getting senile! It might have confirmed their thought that I was nuts all the time they had known me!

I wonder if Dockie is still behind that door. Someone else lives in that house now. Will somebody please look back there for me?

Possibly calling my imaginary friend, "Dockie".

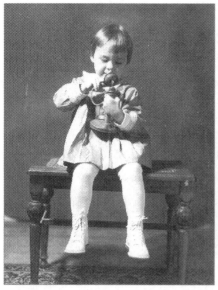 

Other "friends" enjoying a "concert". I can remember that piano. It was green! Check out those leggings. Leggings and long sleeves seemed to be the necessity back in the day. I can remember hating to put on those leggings – Ugh!

Curls, Coveralls and a Brakeman's Cap

During my very early years – and into much later years – the idol for little girls was the precious and beautiful child actress, Shirley Temple, and her glorious head of curls. When she made her debut, her curls were all the rage. Any little girl with a length of hair wanted curls like Shirley's. I was not old enough to follow the hair fashions yet, but my mama was. Mamas wanted their little girls to look like Shirley. I was no exception. However, my curls certainly were not natural. I had the straightest head of hair in our family! So, when my hair had grown long enough, the curls were artificially produced upon my little head by my mama. I really didn't care anyway, and it made my mama happy, so I tolerated the curling process.

One day, after the curling had been done and my mama was busy in the kitchen, I spied her scissors on a table in the living room, where she had inadvertently left them. Uh-Oh! At an early age, I had been well schooled in the art of cutting and being careful with scissors. However my own scissors were the blunt type used by children. Cutting paper dolls didn't require much more than those little scissors had to offer. I had already become proficient with them, cutting out the clothes for my paper dolls. But those long, sharp pointed scissors intrigued me. What could I sneak off and cut with them? (Now, don't get ahead of me.) I knew I had to hide if I wanted to use that adult tool. Those were definitely not kid scissors.

Suddenly a bright idea! I crawled in behind the divan in the living room. (We call them sofas or couches these days.) First I had to hide and then decide what I was going to cut. I knew it would not be a good idea to cut a piece from my clothes. I was barefoot at the time, so I couldn't cut the strings off my shoes. I didn't think it was a good idea to do any damage to the back of the divan, although it did occur to me to cut just a small hole to peek into and see what was inside of it that made it so soft.

Than it hit me! You guessed it – hair. I decided to trim off a little bit of hair. I had a lot of hair and a lot of curls that hung down all over my head.

Surely it wouldn't be noticed if I trimmed off some of it. However, little kids can never be satisfied with just a little bit. I thought if I cut off just one curl, it wouldn't be missed among all the others. So, I selectively snipped off a curl and found out that it was kind of fun to play with. Wrapping it around a little finger after detaching it was fun. Since that was such a good idea, I decided to cut off a curl here and there so that I would have one to wrap around each of my fingers. I convinced myself that nobody would notice them being gone, and it was such fun playing "beauty shop" with them, just kidding around behind the divan.

About that time, my mama discovered I was nowhere in sight, and she began calling me. When I didn't answer, she remembered that I liked to hide behind the divan when we played hide and seek, so she looked behind it. There I was, looking up at her, with pieces of detached hair curled around my fingers and all over the floor around me. Much to my dismay, she also noticed some spots missing from the hair on my head. She shrieked! And I mean shrieked! It wasn't just the hair - that was bad enough. It was the fact that there sat her baby with a pair of sharp scissors in her hand. Taking in that whole picture must have really freaked her out! First she relieved me of the scissors, set them back on the table (where she had left them in the first place – some mamas never learn). From that moment on, it was downhill all the way! I knew I was about to get walloped. She pulled me from behind the divan and swatted my bottom a few good licks. Later, when I looked in the mirror, I knew it was well deserved. But that was not the end of the punishment. I had to sit in the "big chair" in our living room while my mama swept up all the hair from behind the divan and disposed of it – all but one of the "curls", which she put into a little envelope to keep. That "big chair" was timeout for me before timeout even had a name!

After a few minutes, when my mama had regained her composure a bit, she called my daddy and squealed on me. After a few minutes of conversation with my daddy, my mama put my shoes on me and hustled (more like dragged) me out the door and off we went to the barbershop. I am sure the conversation was a joint decision to correct the problem that way. I had to ride the streetcar with mama for a few blocks looking like a badly trimmed hedge on top, much to my embarrassment. It was very noticeable! The barber was the nice man who trimmed my daddy's hair, so I was familiar with him. His name was Mr. Alexander, but since I had always had trouble saying his name perfectly, I called him "Mister Lelander". Mister Lelander took one look at the botched hair and just stared at my mama, trying to hold back a laugh. All she told him was to "shingle" it in the back – that was where the cutting had been done. First, he washed my hair and dried it a little bit and combed it down straight all over. He cut bangs across my forehead, let the sides hang down over my ears, trimmed the hair off just to the ear lobes, and then "shingled" the back. "Shingling" meant cutting graduated lengths from the back of my head, ending up short at the nape of the neck, for those who don't know the term. A similar style was popular back in the 1920s, also, but without the hair down over the ears. Back then; the ladies had little "spit curls" at the sides in front of their ears. Much more stylish than the haircut I was getting. But I guess that was about all that could have been done to correct the mess I had made. I hated it! I looked like Buster Brown (without his little dog). It was so ugly to me that I vowed to never again try to trim my hair.

But that is not the end of the story. I mostly had little boys to play with in our neighborhood on Wilton St., but I didn't want to look like them. I knew however, that I had to live with that haircut for a while, after what I had done. Then, in a few days, I found the solution – a way to hide my shameful hair. On a shopping trip downtown to Dallas, I discovered in one of the shops there a cute "brakeman's cap". That kind of cap has a sort of poofed top, and is made of a striped, pillow ticking material, with a bill in front. My mama let me buy it, and I wore it backward with the bill in back to further hide my ugly haircut. She even let me buy a pair of matching coveralls. A little long in the legs and sleeves, but the smallest size we could find, and we just rolled up the cuffs to expose my shoes and hands. My mama thought they were cute and anyway they were cheap and sturdy play clothes. I fooled her! All I wanted was that big cap to completely envelop my head and hide that hair. The coveralls were just icing on the cake to throw her off the track of discovering the real reason for the cap. At least I thought I fooled her. She was pretty sharp and didn't like the haircut any better than I did. I wore that cap everyday when I was outside, even if I didn't wear the baggy overalls. Punishment lasted until my hair grew back. I never tried to cut it again. Lesson learned!

Definitely not stylish, but it covered the bad
haircut and apparently made me happy!

I can't believe my mama allowed me to purchase this getup. It was, however, the perfect attire for a little prankster.
My daddy probably took this photo to haunt me later.

The Mirror

My mama had a beautiful piece of furniture in my parents' bedroom on Wilton Street. In those days we called it a "vanity". It had raised sides with drawers and beautiful drawer pulls, and between them was a sort of "well" or lower part of the piece. I wish I could describe it better than that, but I imagine you get the idea, or maybe are old enough to have seen one like it. It stood on slender legs and had a pretty upholstered slim legged bench that came with it. There were small mirrors on each side over the raised parts and these mirrors slightly swiveled from side to side to get a better look at oneself. In the middle and standing taller than the other two mirrors was the main mirror that was as wide as the "well" portion of the vanity. My mama had her makeup, hairbrushes and combs in the drawers and there was crocheted doilies on top of the sides and middle portion under her perfume and pretty bottles. These doilies were made by her mother. The vanity was new and the prettiest piece of furniture in the bedroom. My daddy had given it to her as a gift, and she was as proud of it as anything in our house. She kept those mirrors cleaned and shiny and the wood polished to a beautiful sheen. Obviously a cherished and protected piece.

My aunt who lived next door had a daughter That cousin was about ten years older than I was. One of her delights was to tease me when I was three and four years old. When I was three years old and trying to go to sleep on our back screened in porch she would sneak up the driveway between our houses at night and tease me through the screen, by telling me that the man in the moon was watching me. I finally figured that one out and it didn't scare me anymore. Then she would tell me that she saw me hesitate on the corner. It took longer to figure out what that meant. Her best one was when she asked me if I itched, because she knew that I had ancestors. I asked my mama about those words and got an explanation and was able to laugh at my cousin's taunts after that. But there was another method of teasing that she found effective in harassing me. She would push me behind the door of my parents' bedroom (where I kept my imaginary friend Dockie) and pinch me and tell me to stay there with my friend all day. In later years, she was a really good friend to me and I still cannot understand why she was so mean to me when I was little. Maybe it was a jealousy thing because I was the baby girl that got more attention. I'm glad she finally outgrew it, however.

One day when I was roughly shoved behind the bedroom door and pinched, I decided I had had enough! I had been playing with my set of little toy tools when my cousin came into the room. When she grabbed me and pushed me behind the door, I just happened to have a small toy hatchet from the tool set in my hand. After she had me stashed behind the door and was retreating from the room, I came out and hurled the toy hatchet at her. Big mistake! She ducked. The hatchet hit the large mirror on my mama's vanity dead center! It made a big spider web pattern immediately. My cousin saw what happened and sped out our front door so fast that she was just a blur. My mama heard the commotion and came running to the bedroom. I just stood there in shock. I tried to tell my mama what had happened, but she was pretty mad and really wasn't listening. Instead of spanking me for what I had done, she drew up the bench in front of the shattered mirror and sat me down on it and told me to stare at it until I was told to move from that spot. I would rather have had a thrashing! I had to sit there all day long looking at that broken mirror. She even served my lunch there and I ate it off of the well part of the vanity. Of course I cried a lot, but that did not change the punishment. I was only allowed to move to go to the bathroom. Talk about "time out" – we had it before it even had a name!

When my daddy came home from work, there I sat. He took one look at my face and at the broken mirror and didn't even ask what had happened. My mama had cooled off a bit by then, however, and allowed me to come to the dinner table that evening. Guess what the subject was. Temper. Of course, I did get to tell my side of the story and my aunt received a full report about my cousin's bad behavior, also. My parents did not have that mirror repaired right away. I imagine it was partly because it was very expensive and partly because they wanted the lecture about losing one's temper to really sink in every time I looked at that mirror. It worked. No kidding!

Here is a smaller version of "The Mirror", and probably a safer one for me. Actually, what this photo shows is that we females begin at an early age to powder our nose.

(Still can't get rid of those leggings, though!)

The Old Red Rooster

As I mentioned previously, as a child I hated those chickens on the run! Now I will tell you why .

My aunt next door had a large fenced backyard. The fence was not very tall and pretty easy to climb over if you were careful. However, I was warned to never scale that fence or even to enter her backyard through the gate without being accompanied by an adult. The reason for that was that among the chickens my aunt had running allover her backyard was a mean old red rooster that was whacked aside by her on more than one occasion. Just like forbidden fruit that seems to need picking, getting into that backyard alone without being discovered was high on my list of things to accomplish one summer when I was about four years old. After all, I was just kidding around.

While my daddy was at work and my mama was on her way to the grocery store, I was left next door to be watched over by my aunt. In those days it was possible for small children to play outside around the house without being constantly under the watchful eyes of an adult. Nobody perverted ever bothered us back then. So while my aunt was preparing our lunch, I decided to climb over her back fence into her backyard with all those chickens. She would have heard the gate opening, so I took the fence-climbing route. Obviously the plan was to get into the chicken yard without being detected. I crossed the yard and made it all the way to the other side where her garage was located before that bad old rooster saw me and began running toward me.

I was the intruder. He was the chicken police! He ran across the yard at top speed with his wings spread out and his head down and his beak pointed directly toward me! Then he began his attack! He backed me up against the garage and proceeded to fly at me, flapping his wings. While doing that he was attempting to flog me with his sharp claws. I began flailing my arms at him and trying to fight him off, while screaming at the top of my lungs! My aunt came dashing out of her back door to rescue me, but not before that old red rooster had wounded me with some pretty good scratches to my arms and chest. While the rooster was still hopping on me, my aunt grabbed a big bushel basket from the ground nearby and chased that rooster into a comer and popped that basket right down over him. That stopped his attack on me, but you should have seen that basket bounce and slide all over the yard with Mr. Rooster underneath and unable to escape. Looking back, I have to laugh. Just get a mental picture of that bouncing basket and the other chickens running madly around the yard clucking loudly, unable to figure it out. My aunt just left him there all day. She guided me back sobbing into the house. She doctored my wounds and comforted me, and needless to say, I had some delicious tomato soup and crackers with my lunch. Of course there were a few veggies, which had already been prepared, on the side. And after my mama returned from the grocery, she combined her profuse sympathy with a little "I told you so" speech, together with a final warning about not going into the chicken yard and messing with the chickens.

My grandmother also had chickens, but without the mean rooster. I remember going out into her backyard and scattering chicken feed for her flock. Those chickens loved me.

But that's not the end of the red rooster story. That rooster remained an inmate of that basket all day, hovered over by a few hens. The next day was Saturday and my daddy was at home from work. That morning my daddy and my aunt went after that old rooster in her yard and then they …….well…. sparing you the details…. 1 will just say that we all had fried chicken for dinner that night!

Maybe this story has three messages: (1) Don't disobey your family's warnings, (2) if you are a rooster, don't mess with an aunt and her only niece, and (3) all actions have a reaction, and sometimes a bad consequence - even death!

Being a kid, I didn't always pay attention to my parents' warnings, or consider what the consequences could be, but 1 sure didn't go kidding around by myself in the chicken yards again!

Grandmother's Grocery Store – Play Place for a Naughty Child

Since my grandmother lived only a few doors down Wilton Street from our house, I walked down the street by myself to visit her almost daily, even though I was a small child. Her house was a unique place for a kid to visit, because the front room of the house, through the front door, just off of the front porch, was a small grocery store. The rest of the house was her home. It was like most small frame houses in the neighborhood - a square box divided into four spaces with a small bathroom wedged in next to a bedroom. My grandmother's bedroom/sitting room was also at the front of the house next to the grocery store. I loved to play with some of the "what-nots" that she had on shelves in her bedroom. She would carefully take them down from the shelves and let me play with them in the floor while she kept a close eye on me. There were quite a few tiny porcelain dolls and figurines in her collection that perched out of my reach on a couple of corner shelves. Luckily I never broke any of her pretty collectibles. Please take note here that there was no TV set in that room – we hadn't heard of them quite yet, so when I was at my grandmother's house, one of my activities was to play with her little dolls and use my imagination – a lost art today, I am afraid.

Adjacent to her bedroom was my grandmother's bathroom, which was a plain, simple bathroom like they all were back then. Tub, (no shower), toilet, sink, small heater – that was it. It wasn't interesting enough to catch my attention as a place to play. Behind the grocery store area was my grandmother's large, open kitchen. I think it was originally another small bedroom and kitchen, but it had been opened up to be one large room. She had many cabinets around the walls of the kitchen, and they held all sort of things for me to play with. I used to take her pots and pans out of one of the lower cabinets and bang around and play in the floor

35

with them, causing her to wash them all when I left to go home. By the way, there was no dishwasher in her kitchen, or any other home kitchen in those days. She must have loved me dearly to have to wash all those pans by hand in the kitchen sink when I was finished dirtying them in the floor. One particular pan, which she called her "stewer" was a large round pot that, as a small child, I fit into nicely if I pulled my knees up and put my feet in it, as I sat in it. Then I would push against the linoleum floor with my hands and make the pot swirl around in circles. Good grief! What a spoiled grandchild I was! I guess it kept me out of her way for a few minutes, though. She not only had a gas stove in her kitchen, she also had an old black pot-bellied wood burning stove with a flue going up through the roof of the house. She always had a pot of coffee keeping warm on that old black stove in winter, while she burned her little wood logs in it to keep her kitchen warm. In the middle of the kitchen was a big round wooden table, covered with a white tablecloth, which she had made by hand, and several chairs. That's where I often sat to consume a sugar cookie and a glass of milk. She called the cookies "teacakes". They were big around, crisp on the outside and soft in the middle. Anybody remember those? I'll never forget how good they tasted! During those cookie-eating sessions, I also learned to enjoy buttermilk. I know some of you have just said "eewww" or "ugh", but I still love buttermilk. Must be an acquired taste developed along with eating teacakes at an early age.

Just behind the kitchen was the small back porch nook. (More about what went on there in a later chapter.) It was a wonderful little house, and the only one like it in our neighborhood.

Now, back to the grocery store. As you entered the front door of the house, you came directly into the grocery store. In the middle of the room, my grandmother had a cold meat counter – like the ones you have probably seen in old movies – a slanted glass front and shoulder-high white top. I was absolutely forbidden to go into that meat counter under threat of a spanking! I didn't. On top of that meat cooler sat three shallow open boxes, which contained three different types of dried beans. Grandmother also sold a few fresh vegetables from her garden occasionally, and fresh eggs straight from her backyard chickens. She didn't sell milk – we all had a milkman who came to our houses for that. On one long wall, and under the front window, were a few shelves, which contained canned goods and flour and sugar and small amounts of other products. I loved to play there in that little store, and sometimes helped wait on the customers. However, when no customers were around and my grandmother was busy elsewhere in her house, I dragged up a chair and climbed on top of the meat cooler and proceeded to "integrate" those beans. The different colors mixed together looked pretty to me. This only happened a couple of times, and afterward I was made to sit down at the big kitchen table to re-sort the beans into their proper boxes. Needless to say, it took much longer to separate the beans than it did to mix them together, and not nearly as much fun. That was punishment enough for a little four year old who really wanted to run barefoot all over the neighborhood instead of sorting beans.

After the bean episode, I soon found another way to frustrate my grandmother. Since I was my mama's and daddy's only child it seemed to be her duty to suffer that fate when I was around. My next excursion was to another set of shelves that held boxes of several varieties of candy on them. They were on the top shelf out of the reach of little hands from around the neighborhood. Grandmother was not naïve! However, I was able to drag the chair (same one I used to get to the beans) over to the shelves when my grandmother was outside feeding her chickens sometimes. I could barely reach those candy boxes, but I managed to raid them, for only one reason. I wasn't interested in eating some of the candy. I had something else in mind. One of the boxes held bite sized taffy treats, which were wrapped in a sort of waxy tan colored paper. There was then another paper wrapper around them, which was twisted at both ends. Inside that outer wrapper was a small prize, and you didn't know what it was until you bought the candy and opened the twisted ends. Thus the candy's name, "Guess What". Even though the prize was dinky, those were very popular candies with the neighborhood kids. Back then they only cost a penny each. A real bargain in those Great Depression days when penny candy was about all most people could afford.

My first adventure into a life of crime involved those little candies. By now I am sure you are way ahead of me, and I don't know why I never thought of it before. When no one was around to see what I was doing, I would drag up my partner-in-crime chair, climb up on it and take a couple of taffy treats from the box each time and unwrap the outer paper. Then I would remove the prizes, re-wrap the candy, twisting it at both ends, and replace it in the box. No one was the wiser for a while, until the neighborhood kids began complaining that they didn't get their prize with their "Guess Whats". It wasn't long before my grandmother got wise to what was going on. I think her first clue to who was robbing the prizes from the candy was when she remembered frequently finding the chair sitting next to the candy shelf. Right away she put two and two together. After more threats of bottom spanking, that was my last attempt at petty theft.

When my aunt bought another house and moved from our neighborhood, my grandmother retired and moved in with her. She had a little notebook in her grocery store, which held the list of customers who had been forced to ask for credit to buy their food from her. That my grandmother was willing to do this was a blessing to many people in the area, during the Great Depression, when some had lost jobs and had little money with which to buy food. She was generous to a fault sometimes, and was left with a lot of debts that some of these folks were never able to repay. She just couldn't make herself turn anyone away empty handed. She had aged by then, also, and keeping that store was becoming a burden to her, so she closed the credit book and forgave all those debts, sold her house and moved away with my aunt. I missed being able to trot down the street to grandmother's house and store, as well as to my aunt's house next door, but it wasn't very long after they moved away that my daddy and mama bought our new house a few blocks away from where my aunt and grandmother lived. By then I was old enough to be able to ride my bike that few blocks and visit them occasionally, so it wasn't a total loss to me. I was in elementary school by then and busy with other things. Life was changing and getting better for most folks by the time we all moved from the old neighborhood, and I had, and still have, all those wonderful memories of spending my very early childhood years back there on Wilton Street.

Grandmother's Front Porch

I have described my grandmother's house and my escapades in her grocery store. Now, let me tell you what a great place her front porch was for a doted on child.

One very popular soft drink in my early days was RC Cola. The reason it was so popular was because it was the biggest bottle. Kids aren't stupid. In those days you tried to get all you could for your nickel, and kids didn't get many nickels to spend on junk food back then. My grandmother stocked bottles of that drink in her front porch cooler – all iced down and ready to enjoy. The cooler was a large metal box-type appliance with four short legs and a lid covering the top. The lid had hinges in the middle and folded back to expose the contents inside. It in no way resembled the soft drink cooling and dispensing machines of today, into which you insert your coins and press a button for you choice. The box on my grandmother's porch was a self-help drink dispenser which also had a ripple-edged bottle opener attached to one side. There were no canned soft drinks in those days. We all drank out of glass bottles with caps that had to be removed by a bottle opener.

After a customer selected a drink, they walked into the front room grocery store area and paid my grandmother for the drink. Being a frequent visitor as well as her grandchild, I just selected my drink and went into the house to pick up my little bag of peanuts, without a thought of paying for them. Then I returned to the porch, perched on the high backed bench beside the drink box, ready to enjoy my between meal treat. The preparation of this treat was so simple a child – like me – could do it. Just flip the top off the bottle and dispose of it in the little bucket beside the drink box under the bottle opener. You did not throw the caps into the front yard, and everybody knew it. Then, sitting on the bench, I opened my little pack of peanuts. No, you didn't eat the peanuts out of the package; you poured the whole packet very carefully into the small bottle top of the soda. After all the nuts were in the bottle, you swirled them around a few times, turned up the bottle to your mouth and enjoyed a sip of cola with a small bite of nuts. I just sat there enjoying that treat until it all was gone. Since empty glass bottles brought a one-cent refund, you took them back to the source from where they were purchased for your refund. There were no plastic bottles back then. Of course I never had to worry about the refund, because I never paid for it in the first place. I just gave the bottle back to grandmother along with a hug and kiss.

Although my grandmother's front porch was a cool and shady place for me to stop playing a while and indulge myself in treats, it also overlooked a yard that sloped down to the main sidewalk. At one corner of the downward sloping yard where it met the main sidewalk, my grandmother had built a little rock garden. A pretty little place, but one that proved to be dangerous one afternoon after I had indulged in my treat and was departing the yard. That day, on my way back to play with my neighbors, I stopped at that little garden spot long enough to "rearrange" some of the rocks in the flowerbed, as I frequently did for amusement. When I lifted one of the larger rocks, a great big spider hopped out from under it! It was a tarantula! A big old black hairy thing! I was only about four years old and had never heard of a tarantula, but I immediately knew he was not my friend. I just froze to the spot on the sidewalk. I could not make my feet move, but I screamed as loud as I could for my grandmother. The spider kept hopping around the flowerbed. I think he was just trying to scare me away, and if I could have moved, I would have. I simply couldn't make my feet move and just kept screaming until my grandmother came rushing down the steps, along with a couple of neighbors who heard me yelling. My grandmother had apparently been sweeping, since she had a broom in her hand when she came running. She shoved me out of the way and began trying to swat at the spider while he continued jumping around the flowerbed. I still had the rock in my hand for some reason, so my grandmother abandoned the broom and took the rock away from me. By that time the spider had begun to hop on down the sidewalk. She chased after him and flung the rock at him and hit him dead center, sending him to wherever spiders go after life. I just sat down on the sidewalk, still shaking. Afterward, as my grandmother scooped up the dead spider in a sack to dispose of him, I began to feel sorry for him, poor old guy. But then after my grandmother explained to me about how bad a tarantula bite could be, I changed my mind and forgot about being sympathetic.

I ran home and told my mama about the incident. She wasn't sympathetic either. The next day, when I went to visit my grandmother, all the rocks had been turned over and rearranged. I sure was glad, but after that episode with the tarantula, I gave that little flower bed a wide berth each time I passed it.

Grandmother's Back Porch and Making Butter

My grandmother's back porch held a fascination for me. It was a very small covered area just outside her kitchen door. There was no door or screen – just a cozy, fresh air nook. That is where she churned her butter, and I occasionally had the privilege of turning and pumping the churn, while sitting on a little stool beside her. Yes, she had all the amenities (of that time) in her home, such as indoor plumbing, electricity, gas stove, and running water from the tap in the sink, and took advantage of all the up-to-date things that could be purchased, but my grandmother still liked to churn her own butter. I don't imagine it was really fun for her – more like work, but it sure was fun for me! We took turns at the churn and talked about all sorts of things going on around the neighborhood and the world. In the summer, we had our glasses of iced tea sitting next to us and an occasional cookie to go with them. My delight was sticking a finger in the butter when it was about finished and smearing it on a sugar cookie to eat. I even liked just plain licking the sweet fresh butter off of my fingers. What a lost art the churning of fresh butter has become. Another lost art for some of today's families that I had the good fortune of enjoying, was chatting with my grandmother and absorbing her wisdom and knowledge while we churned her butter and ate her cookies. That was also true of sitting around the kitchen table at dinner, talking about my day with my mama and daddy and hearing about theirs, as well as taking advantage of my aunt's academic knowledge while visiting with her at her house. Parents and family members seemed to have had more time for kids back then. That probably helped turn out the responsible group that was my generation

Another creative activity that I enjoyed doing was with my mama at our kitchen table "making butter". This was not done with a churn, however. This wasn't really butter; it was actually fake butter, better known as margarine. You know, kind of like what we enjoy today. However, that margarine back then required a little more work, other then flipping off the lid of a container and dipping into it. And you even had to provide your own container. That butter came in a rectangular refrigerated package that looked like a white block of lard. Also in the package was a small packet of some golden-orange colored powdery stuff. You had to soften the white chunk in a large bowl. After it was sufficiently softened, you sprinkled the power over it and mixed it into the white goo. It was also necessary to keep mushing and mixing it until it had achieved the uniform yellow color of real butter. I stood on a chair and leaned over our bowl on our kitchen table to do the mixing. I had to make sure my hands were sufficiently washed and clean, and then I stuck them into the margarine and squished the stuff with my fingers to help mix in the color. Then I was allowed to scrape my finger around the side of the bowl and like off the margarine. Mmmm, good. But not nearly as sweet as the real thing from my grandmother's churn. After the mixing was finished, my mama would form it into a large ball in her hands and sort of pat it into the original rectangular size. We had a covered butter dish that it fit into nicely after she had it formed to that size. Then back into the refrigerator it went to form solid block of margarine. I still have that butter dish, but it is empty now, while my margarine sits in a plastic container in my own refrigerator. The powder we mixed into that margarine back then probably had some flavoring in it, but the real reason to mix it into the white stuff was to make it actually look like butter. I imagine you could have sliced and eaten it just like it came from the package in the first place as a white block, but it didn't look like butter, so we all mixed in the colored powder to fool ourselves into thinking we were actually eating the real thing.

It didn't take as long to mix that fake butter in a bowl as it did to produce the real thing in my grandmother's churn, and it was not as much work. It was even a lot of fun to squish that creamy stuff between my fingers, but nothing could replace that churning experience, the sweet taste of real butter and the chats with my grandmother on her little back porch.

Running Away To Auntie's House & Tomato Soup

When my mama and I had a disagreement about something, like staying indoors out of the heat or sitting to eat what she had prepared for lunch. I would stretch up to my full kid size and threaten to run away from home. This happened many times because I just loved tomato soup and crackers for lunch. Since I was sort of a skinny little kid, everyone was always trying to put some meat on my bones, and tomato soup alone just wasn't doing that.

When the disagreement concerned "what's for lunch" and it wasn't tomato soup, I ran away next door to my aunt's house. Here is how it went: As soon as I ran to my room to pack my stuff for the trek next door, my mama would call my aunt on the phone in the other room and quietly tell her I would be on the way over there soon. She would then meet my aunt at the back fence and pass my plate of lunch over the fence to her and then run back into the house to help me "pack" for my trip. (I never knew she left the house to do that.) She then escorted me to the door and waved goodbye to me and I began my stroll next door with my little overnight case. All the while, my aunt was heating a pan of tomato soup, which was all ready to eat when I pecked on her door to announce my arrival. She gave me the usual hugs and kisses and said she could see by my overnight case that I had left home for a while. She then told me she was glad I had arrived at just that moment because she had just finished her lunch and had just enough left over for me to have a meal. She always asked me if I would like some soup with my lunch, since she just happened to have some on the stove. So, I had a small cup of tomato soup and a couple of crackers, with a side order of a plate full of meat and veggies, or whatever my mother had prepared that day.

I thought I was a pretty smart kid that couldn't be hoodwinked by any adult hocus-pocus, but for some reason, I never found them out about the over-the-fence-plate-passing charade! Probably one reason I didn't catch on to their deception was that my aunt would scrape whatever my mama prepared off of one of our plates and onto one of her plates. How clever was that! I don't know how they managed to come up with such an elaborate scheme to make me eat properly, without me finding out, but those two sisters knew all about child psychology before it had a name or a fee! It wasn't until years later that they let me in on their good-for-me deception. What even brought up the subject later was the fact that I actually eventually progressed to the point of liking vegetables. However, I still did not have time to sit down and spend a few minutes eating, and I was still skinny. But my mama had noticed that I liked raw veggies, like carrots, radishes, cut up turnips, etc. So at that point she always kept a bowl of ice water in the refrigerator filed with cut up raw veggies of all kinds, and I was encouraged to pop into the house at any time between games and outdoor activities and grab a handful of raw veggies to eat on the run. Again, another clever idea of my mama's to help nourish a skinny kid, whose priority was not eating, just kidding around instead. I guess it is all about how you approach a situation. It worked!

My Auntie holding me,
standing between our two houses.

Grandad's Farm

My daddy's father and mother lived on a farm in East Texas when I was a small child. We visited there, about 70 miles from our home, for family get-togethers with my grandparents and others of my daddy's family. He had four brothers and two sisters. One sister was a schoolteacher, one sister was an entertainer and singer, one brother was an engineer, one brother was a preacher, and the other two brothers were entertainers and singers, also. One of them was even in the old western movies and has a star on the Beverly Hills Walk of Stars. More about those two later. Quite a diverse family group. And they all grew up on my grandad's farm in East Texas.

One of my earliest memories was climbing into our Ford car with running boards and driving off to the country for a visit to Grandad's farm. There were no car seats for kids in those days. I just sat on my mama's lap for the trip. As I recall, I was somewhere in the neighborhood of three years old for my first memory of the visit to the farm.

My grandparents lived in a white frame house with lots of trees in front. The two dogs that ran loose around the farm were named "Bowser" and "Diddy-bite-cha". Don't ask me why. I don't know and never thought to ask. I was too young. The inside of the house was what I would call a typical farmhouse, with a living room at the front on one side and bedrooms along the other side. There was a hall down the middle. Yes, they also had indoor plumbing when I visited them. At the back of the house was the kitchen with a large black cook stove. The biscuits that my grandmother took out of it were huge! There was a large table in the kitchen where everyone sat down to eat. Beside the kitchen was a screened porch that had a round brick wall in the middle, which contained a well. Imagine that – an indoor well. I loved to watch them draw up a bucket of water from the well and let me scoop out a drink of that cool water with a long handled ladle

One of the most unusual treats that my grandmother provided was a taste of fresh watermelon right in the field. She would take my older cousins, and me, barefoot of course, out to the watermelon patch and my grandmother would thump on some watermelons to find a good ripe one. When she found one to satisfy her as to ripeness, she would burst open a ripe melon – with her fist! Takes a good strong farmwoman to do that. But she was a tall, strong and robust woman, so the watermelon was no match for her. Then she pulled the watermelon open, exposing the bright pink center. We kids just reached in with our hands and pulled out pieces of the center, or "heart" as she called it. I learned how to slurp down the delicious treat, while the juice ran down my little fingers and arms onto my clothes. Needless to say, my mama was not on board for this mess, but she always brought along several changes of clothing for me. She was fully aware that farms are not really tidy places for kids to play. My cousins even taught me how to spit out the watermelon seeds toward each other. I learned that feat quickly and really enjoyed the fruity mess in my little hand. After we had finished with one melon, my grandmother would move on down the patch and burst open another one. She would do this until we had all had our fill. When we were finished with our melon eating, the chickens, who had followed us out to the patch, would clean up the rest of the melon. What simple fun and it was so delicious!

Another treat at the farm was the deep creek at the back of the property. I didn't get to go down there often and never alone, because of my young age. But I did get to go with the adults and cousins sometimes to watch them fish. I wasn't old enough to catch a fish by myself, so most of the time when the fishing was going on, I stayed back at the farmhouse. I wasn't disappointed, though, because I liked to watch my grandmother cook on that big old black stove in the kitchen anyway. It was a great delight to sample those fresh foods and delicious ham that came from that farm kitchen, provided by the labor of my grandparents. One of grandmother's biscuits was almost a meal in itself, but the slice of ham and fresh corn on the cob smeared with butter could not be matched anywhere. All that was washed down with fresh milk from their cow or sweet water from their well. Are you hungry yet?

Now, let's get back to that well on the back porch. A hole had been cut in the plank floor of the porch and the brick wall rose up out of the hole, taller than I was at the time. Underneath all that was a very deep brick-sided well which contained the best water I ever tasted. Above the well wall was a wooden frame that peaked and held a rope on a pulley, with a bucket at the end of the rope. The procedure to get the water was to lower the bucket far enough down into the well to get it. Then you cranked up the rope on the pulley until the bucket reached the top rim of the well wall. With the bucket perched there you dipped a shiny metal dipper, which looked like a large long handled spoon, into the bucket and got yourself a sweet, cool drink of well water. The dipper hung on a hook by the well for everyone to use. There weren't any germs lurking around on anyone's mouth in those days, apparently. Needless to say, I was not allowed to play around the well when no adult was around, although a wooden lid was placed atop the well when the well was not in use for drawing water. I guess they had already discovered I had learned to climb at an early age!

My granddad had an old palomino colored horse in his barn. My cousins were all old enough to ride him, but I had to have help. My daddy's sister who taught school had three boys and a girl, all older than I was. My granddad would line us all up on the back of the horse – oldest at the back and holding the reins, next was a cousin in front of him, then me, and up front was another cousin. They were assigned to keep me from falling off the old horse. There we were, four kids crammed together, perched on the gentle old horse, riding bareback. His back was so wide that my legs stuck out straight on either side! It wasn't very comfortable! My largest cousin guided the horse around the back yard and sometimes he would guide him under a big pear tree away from the house. The cousins would pick pears from the tree as we rode under it, and we would eat them while riding horseback. There was one incident, however, that wasn't so much fun when we did that. The pears were not yet ripe enough to be eaten, so we all got a tummy ache and had to lie down and rest a while. We missed dinner that day, needless to say. We didn't do that again.

What a great place for a kid to visit, especially a little city kid. We just had fun playing around in a different environment from where we lived. We didn't have horses or watermelon patches in our neighborhood at home. I am sure farm life was pretty demanding for my grandparents, especially during the Great Depression, but it provided a pleasant escape for the rest of us.

Once, when my mama and daddy took me to visit my grandparents by ourselves, with no other family there for me to play with, I began to pay attention to what my granddad was putting into his mouth and chewing. It was something that came in a small rectangular "brick". He would bite off a piece of it, wrap the rest back in the package and lay it on the table in the hall. I also noticed that he spit a lot and had a cup to catch it. It fascinated me. So, when my parents and grandparents were all out on the porch visiting and drinking iced tea, I disappeared into the house and found the package of tasty looking chocolate-brown stuff. I took it into the bathroom and bit off a piece. I attempted to chew it and then spit. That didn't work for me, however, and I swallowed a bit of it before getting rid of my mouthful of tobacco into the toilet. Oh, my goodness, it was awful! How could my grandad put that stuff in his mouth, much less keep it there and chew on it? I quickly flushed it, cleaned my mouth out, wrapped up the plug and put it back on the hall table. I didn't feel very good for a while and decided it was naptime early that day. They kept feeling of my head to see if I had a fever, but they never did discover why I wasn't hopping around as usual.

My granddad also smoked a pipe. It is a wonder he lived to be over 90 years old, with all that tobacco in his body. But he did and was a sharp old guy right up to the end. He made that pipe-smoking look as good as that tobacco chewing looked to me. I was just too young at the time to associate them as being the same thing. He would puff and puff on his pipe while getting it lit, then blow out a cloud of smoke and sit back and look so happy and relaxed. He also kept his pipe on a stand on the hall table. I imagine you have already guessed what I did on our next visit. Yep, when he rested his pipe on the stand after smoking it for a while, and the family went out into the yard to inspect a new crop of something, I sneaked into the house and retrieved the pipe from its stand and took it into the bathroom. It had not gone out yet, but was just about to and was at the end of the tobacco it held. I stood in front of the bathroom mirror and sucked in a mouthful of smoke, choked, and swallowed some of it, just like I had done with the tobacco juice. I recovered in a minute and quickly replaced the pipe on the table where I had found it. Then I slowly made my way outside to sit on the back porch steps. About that time the family returned to the house, and my grandad came over and gave me a hug. I am sure he smelled the odor of the pipe on me and knew what I had done. I was also very quiet, which should have been a clue to bad behavior. I guess he thought the joke was on me, because he never gave away my secret. He did, however, go back into the house and then returned to the yard smoking his pipe. He looked straight at me, but never said a word. He knew, but I don't think anyone else ever did. I have always wondered if he left that pipe there for me to find, after he noticed I was watching him with so much interest while he smoked it. Kids just don't realize that adults have eyes in the back of their heads and are usually a step ahead of them. Without a doubt, I left the pipe alone after that incident.

One of the last visits to my grandad's farm was a very sad one. My grandmother was very ill and was not expected to live. The whole family was there at the house at her bedside. However, I was too young to be included in the group in her room. I was told to sit in the living room and look at a book. I did for a few minutes, but curiosity got the best of me and I ventured out into the hallway and put my ear next to the bedroom door. What I heard was my grandmother saying something about the beautiful music she was hearing. There was no music playing. She was apparently being welcomed into Heaven. This also frightened me a bit, so I retreated to the living room and waited until the weeping family came out of her room. It was my first experience of someone dear to us passing away. But, you know what, it was apparently a peaceful time for her, with all the angels singing to her as she passed. At least that is what I have always thought.

We didn't go back to the farm much after that. My grandad later moved away to live with his daughter who was the schoolteacher. I remember visiting him there at her house and hearing him sing with some of the others in the family. What a strong bass voice that skinny little man had! He was such a fine old guy. What a legacy he left for his kids. They all had beautiful singing voices and a lot of musical talent, and some made a good living doing so. They all had my grandad's longevity, and they all lived into their late eighties and nineties. Being raised on an East Texas farm sure seemed to agree with every one of them. I hope I also inherited my grandad's longevity genes.

Cars

There were very few cars driving down the streets in our neighborhood. Cars were relatively expensive way back during the Great Depression. My parents had a black Ford when I was about two years old. I believe it was a Model A Ford. I have a photo of myself standing inside of it looking out the window. We had this car for several years – one of the two or three cars in our neighborhood. I also have a photo of me between four and five years old standing with one foot on the ground and the other foot propped on the running board of the car. I was dressed in a pair of Hoot Gibson chaps a Hoot Gibson western shirt and a cowboy hat, playing a Bob Burns bazooka. Hoot Gibson was a popular western movie star back then, and Bob Burns was a countrified comedic entertainer in the 1930s. Burns played an instrument (if you could call it that) called a "bazooka". It was a sort of horn that made sounds like a tissue paper over a comb makes when you blow into it. You could play a tune on it and I used to play the song "I'm An Old Cowhand From The Rio Grande" It went on to say "But my legs ain't bowed and my cheeks ain't tan. I'm a cowboy who never saw a cow, never roped a steer and I don't know how, and I sure ain't fixing to start it now. Yipee-aiyo-kyaa!" Not exactly your current rapper-type music. My family was really into country-western things back then because two of my daddy's brothers were in the country-western music-movie-entertainment business. But more about them later.

The automobiles when I was a small child had stick shifts on the floor. They did not have seat belts of any form. The seats were straight across benches in both back and front. The dashboard held very few instruments, Of course there was no air conditioning or heaters in those old Fords. We just dressed warmly in the winter and rode with the windows shut. In hot weather we dressed lightly while driving and rode with the windows wide open blowing the sometimes hot air around in the car. I say blessings upon the folks who came up with the technology that gave us heating and especially cooling systems in our vehicles!

Some cars had "rumble seats". Those were in the back of the vehicle and opened out backward to expose a couple of padded seats. These were all open-air cars primarily used by the younger set for dating purposes. Very wind-blown seating. I don't know where the name came from, but I imagine since they were right out in the open there was a lot of rumbling sounds all around those backend pull-out seats. Our car had a small trunk in back, but nothing like the larger trunks of today, which can hold something as large as a folded up wheelchair.

I know two things about automobiles back then: First, the gasoline used to run them was very, very, even extremely inexpensive even for depression times. (I remember a sign saying 15 cents per gallon.) Second, there was no government donation in the billions of dollars to the automakers. Somehow the marketplace took over, and people are still driving automobiles. It worked back then! I guess history has a good lesson - - if we pay attention, that is.

Whee! I love this car, even if it does need washing.

No, I am not shooting you a bird.
I am just happy to be out of those leggings and barefoot!
(Ugh! What a dirty running board!)

The Driving Lesson

Almost everyday my daddy drove our car to work, but one day he decided he would ride the streetcar to work and leave the car at home sitting in the driveway. I don't know why he left it there, and I also don't know why my mama decided it was time for her to learn to drive. Big mistake! My daddy had shown her the steps to follow as he was driving and apparently she thought driving back and forward up and down our driveway would be a good way to practice driving. Thank goodness she didn't attempt it on the street!

Back in those days, the cars had floor-mounted stick shifts with a knob handle on top. The driver held the knob and moved the stick shift forward, backward or to the left or right to shift into the proper gear. There were also three pedals that had to be worked with the feet. While maneuvering the stick into the proper position, it was also necessary for the driver to press the left foot down on the far left floor pedal, called the clutch. At the same time the driver then pressed down with the right foot on the far right pedal, which was the accelerator or "gas pedal", as the left pedal was gradually released, causing the car to move either forward or backward. The middle pedal was the brake pedal. I know all this not only because my daddy showed me, but also because many years later, I learned to drive a car with clutch, brake and accelerator pedals lined up on the floor like that. The only difference was that the stick shift had moved up next to the steering wheel by then. I'm sure many of you readers remember those old cars of the 1930s and 1940s, also. Today's cars are so easy to operate that that it makes one of those oldies seem like a nightmare to drive. In my mama's case, it sure was!

Right away, as soon as she got behind the wheel of the car, she did all the steps necessary to drive the car forward – right into the closed garage doors! Our garage was detached from the house and held only one car. It had two doors – a left and a right side – that met in the middle with a place where you hung a lock. After the first forward move by my mama, our garage doors formed a V-shape in the middle pointing toward the back of the garage, swinging the wrong way on their hinges, with the broken lock hanging off one of them. After this move, she immediately shifted the car into reverse, after again following all the steps with her feet and hands. This time she backed up - right into my aunt's back fence next to our driveway, laying that fence almost to the ground and traumatizing a yard full of my aunt's chickens! Apparently, during this entire attempt at learning to drive, my mama never thought to use the brake pedal! The downed fence blocked her exit from the driver's side of the car, so she took out the keys and slid over and out of the passenger side of the car and started quickly back into the house, leaving the car sitting where it stopped.

I watched this lesson from our back-screened porch. When she began to head back to the house, I quickly ran out our front door and over to my aunt's house. As I was crossing our driveway on the way to her house, I saw her standing there, looking at her fallen fence and shaking her head. Those two ladies didn't discuss the problem right then, and I quickly took off in another direction, just in case they decided to chat over the fence. When my daddy came home from work, there was, of course a family discussion which included some input from my aunt. The next day was Saturday, so my daddy was at home for the day. He removed the car from my aunt's fence and repaired and replaced the broken section, while the chickens watched and squawked at him. Then he went to buy new hinges for the garage doors and repaired them. I can't remember what the damage was to the car or how, or if, it was ever repaired. The fallen fence and garage doors were enough drama for me to remember.

Bless my mama's heart. She was the sweetest, most precious lady, and a perfect mama. She just was not cut out to be a driver. That fateful day, my mama swore never to try to drive a car again – and she never did.

Ouchies!

As a small kid I guess I had my share of small wounds and hurts known to me as "Ouchies". I seemed to always have a bandage wrapped around my big toe on one foot or the other due to stubbing it while running barefoot down the sidewalks or playing hopscotch. Knee scrapes were very common among our kidding around set, also. In warm weather, kids went barefoot back then. I guess it saved our shoes for when we needed to dress up, like going to church. Shoes were expensive back then. I just liked the free feeling of going barefoot, and was willing to put up with the occasional toe stubbing due to a bit of clumsiness. We kids probably had the toughest feet of anyone, and blisters only came with wearing shoes. Those heel blisters were covered with adhesive bandage strips until they healed. We didn't even seem to mind the hot sidewalks.

There was always a chalked hopscotch game on our front sidewalk. Sometimes we just used white rocks to draw a long series of hopscotch squares. We also used our drawing instruments to decorate the sidewalks with our kid art, but crayons were forbidden on sidewalks. That wouldn't wash off. My major drawback in hopscotch was the toe stubbing. Wearing shoes would have eliminated that problem, of course. But that just wasn't my thing in summer. Today the very thought of running anywhere barefoot, much less on a hard sidewalk, makes my feet begin to ache.

One day while going without shoes, I really suffered a bad wound to my foot, running where I should not have gone. That barefoot incident that I will never forget happened at about age 4 . It came close to convincing me to wear shoes year around. Here is what happened:

While hopping around barefoot playing in a vacant lot in our neighborhood, I stepped on a rusty nail which was attached to a small piece of wood, just hard enough to drive it upward and out through the top of my little foot. I hopped home on he other foot screaming for my mama, and she came running. When she saw what had happened, she quickly called the doctor. In those days, doctors would come to the house to cure your ills or in case of an accident. Before our doctor came that day, he gave my mama instructions to find some kerosene and put it in a deep pan or bucket and submerge my foot in it, nail, wood and all. He told her not to remove the nail until he arrived at our house. Somewhere, I don't know where, she rounded up a pan full of kerosene and dunked my throbbing foot into it. Back then kerosene was used for some cleaning projects, so I imagine my mama did not have to look far to find some. She did find some and dunked my foot in it. The doctor arrived a few minutes later and gave me something that "relaxed" me, and with the foot still submerged in the kerosene, pulled out the nail and wood. Then he cleaned the wound, dressed it and gave me a tetanus shot. Afterward I took a very long nap. The foot was petty sore for a few days and I had to stay on our front porch and away from the dirt and grass until the doctor looked at my foot again and determined that it was healing. I had to wear a thick sock on that foot for a while, but still hopped barefoot around the house on he other foot. However, I was very careful after that episode to stay away from hopping around in vacant lots with their bits of dangerous debris!

Another "ouchie" happened right in our own bathroom. Our bathroom was the typical 1930s arrangement. Tub free standing off the floor on 4 claw feet, plain sink, plain toilet- all white, of course – and a small white electric heater sitting off to the side across from the tub. The one bathroom in the house was adjacent to my mama and daddy's bedroom. When I was about three years old, after my bath, and after my mama had dried me off, she was hanging the towel on a towel rod, turning her back for a split second. That was just enough time for me to take a seat on top of the heater. Ouch! Since I put my hands back behind me and down first on the heater, my bottom just grazed it. But I scorched palms of both hands. I screamed bloody murder, of course, immediately getting my mama's attention. Due to my many "ouchies", we had plenty of medications in the bathroom medicine cabinet, and she quickly grabbed one of them and smeared something greasy over both my palms and loosely wrapped my hands with gauze. She was in action before I hardly had time to feel the pain and all healed in a few days. It was a little difficult trying to feed myself for a while, but I didn't really like to eat anyway and my mama helped me. Needless to say, I never went near that old white heater again, whether it was on or not! Live and learn!

Now let's go back outside for more dangerous kidding around. When I wasn't running up and down the sidewalk I was doing a lot of tree climbing. One particular tree across the street had one fairly low limb. Just above it was another limb about two feet higher and aimed out in the same direction. One summer day I climbed onto the lower limb and then hung by my hands and swung back and forth. After that there was a drop to the ground, followed again by climbing back onto that limb, swinging back and forth with my body hanging fully down and feet a few feet off of the ground. This was going just fine, as usual, until one of the newer neighborhood boys, who were older and taller than I was, decided to climb up the tree onto the limb above mine. This created the problem. He held onto the higher branch and then let his body drop down and began to swing as he had seen me do. I was on the lower limb and stretched fully out toward the ground just ready to drop. Too late! Before I could drop out of his way, here he came swinging toward me at full throttle with feet extended. Those feet connected solidly with the pit of my stomach sending me tumbling to the ground with the breath knocked right out of me!. My aunt was watching us play from her front window across the street and immediately came running to my rescue. I was gasping for breath and so woozy at that point that I couldn't even get up off the ground. There I lay with the boy hovering over me saying he was sorry over and over again, I think he thought he had killed me. But my aunt knew what to do and had me sitting up and breathing and eventually standing in no time. She said later that her experiences as an elementary school teacher for many years made her an expert on the subject of playground mishaps and breath knocked out of children. It's obviously a kid thing.

Getting the breath knocked out of me only happened one other time, years later when I was in elementary school. I was on the school playground acting as catcher in a girls' softball game. A batter hit the ball, I stood up, she slung the bat backward right into my midsection and down I went gasping for breath. At least it didn't hit me in the head. I survived that hit, also, but with a large knot and a bruise. Yes, I am convinced it is a kid thing. You can get hurt pretty bad sometimes when you are just "kidding around", and I was not finished falling out of trees. The same summer that I had the breath knocked out of me while playing in a tree, I didn't get the message and climbed up onto a branch of the China Berry tree in the front yard of the house on the corner. This tree limb was about 5 feet off of the ground, stuck out several feet horizontally, and was wide enough for a small kid to sit on while hanging onto a branch above it. I had done that many times while eating popsicles. Don't ask me why that was my place to eat them. Only a kid would know to do that. I also loved to sit on that limb and just sing and be happy watching the world go by on a summer afternoon. It was a nice shady place to be.

One afternoon I was sitting in that tree sucking on a Popsicle and staying cool. No air conditioned houses in those days, so you might as well stay outside somewhere in the shade. As I relaxed on my limb, a bumblebee decided to light on my Popsicle. How dare he do that! I flung it away as far as I could throw it while clinging to my tree limb. But that old bee wasn't having any of that. He wasn't finished with me yet. I guess I made him mad by not sharing my treat with him, and he flew away and circled around and flew back toward me. I batted at him and he flew away again. But little did I know that he flew behind me, landed behind my right ear and delivered his big bumblebee sting. It knocked me right out of that tree yelling and crying! It is a wonder I didn't break something falling out of that tree, but luckily I didn't. Right away here came both my mama and my aunt running across the yards to see what I had done to myself that time. By then I was sitting flat on the ground holding my ear. I can remember screaming to them "Bee!" They took me into our house and put a plaster of dampened baking soda behind my ear to ease the pain. It was not fun, believe me, and I had a small swollen knot behind my ear very quickly. I have had wasp sings several times over the years, but that bumblebee sting was one that lives on in my memory as the worst! And I'm not kidding.

There is one thing worse than a bumblebee sting, however. One Fourth of July my daddy was letting me play with some of those little sparklers out on our front walk. After I was finished, I went to sit on the front porch to watch the other neighbors doing all sorts of small fireworks. It didn't seem to be against the law in those days to do that in neighborhoods. In a few minutes I was standing up leaning on a porch post not paying attention to what my daddy was doing, when he decided he would shoot off a firecracker in the driveway out of my sight. It scared me and I hopped off of the porch to the ground...right onto a scorpion! Of course I was barefooted – I was always barefooted. . It killed the scorpion when I landed on him, but not before he delivered his venom right into my heel. That was the end of my July 4th celebrating, believe me. I knew right than what is worse than a bumble bee sting.. You don't want to monkey around with those stinging scorpions, not even the small household varieties. Those little guys don't kid around!

All of the preceeding were ouchies that I can remember experiencing at a very early age. However in a chapter coming up later I will describe the worst injury of my entire life. It was also sustained when I was just "kidding around". Sometimes being a kid is a dangerous job! Keep reading…..

The Nail Trick

My daddy was a body builder and was Director of the Dallas YMCA Health Club when I was a small child. He was very muscular and firm and well built and apparently thought everyone else should be the same. He really worked at being healthy and strong. Even to the day he had his first heart attack, he was assisting men to learn weight lifting and bodybuilding. In his 60s at the time, lifting a weight to teach someone how it was done was a real feat! He did survive that attack, however. I have said all that to illustrate how strong that sweet loveable man was.

When I was about four years old, I discovered a talent that my daddy had that few people could accomplish. I saw him do the trick at a weight lifting meet one time and it stuck in my mind. One day I had the good idea of inviting my neighborhood friends on Wilton St. to come to our backyard and watch my daddy drive a nail through a one inch pine board laid across a couple of saw horses. Not out of the ordinary? Oh, yes, it was. After the crowd had gathered, my daddy would fold a handkerchief into the palm of his hand. He then held a 3 inch nail in the hand covered by the handkerchief, drew back his hand over his head, and then with a powerful and fast downward motion, he drove that nail right through the board! He frequently did this exhibition of strength and concentration at several weight lifting meets for several years. I guess this accomplishment was some cousin to the current day Karate strength and concentration displays, such as breaking boards or concrete blocks with a person's hand. I never did find out where he learned to do this nail trick or why. I was just in awe of anyone who could do a thing like that and not come up with a wound to their palm. All my little playmates and the folks at the weight lifting meet were also impressed. What a guy he was!

Christmases Past

During the Great Depression years, if kids received nice toys at all, it was probably just at Christmas. In my case, I guess I was luckier than most kids, because my daddy had a decent job and my parents could afford to give their only child a few nice gifts occasionally. But we were also impacted by the depression financially, so most of my own gifts came at Christmas. Since my birthday was exactly one month after Christmas, I had a sort of split gifting result, with the larger presents given at Christmas. Actually, I can't seem to remember what my birthday gifts were way back then. But some of the Christmas presents are still very vivid in my mind.

One of my Christmas gifts when I was about four years old was a little table just my size, with two chairs to match. (See photo.) If you can imagine it, I still have that table and chairs to this day! I have toted them around or stored them for all these years waiting for my grandchildren. When my son was old enough to use them, my husband and I painted them brown and put decals suited to a boy on them. After he outgrew the chairs, we stored them and waited for more children to enjoy them. Sure enough, when my daughter was old enough, we took the little table and two chairs out of storage, repainted them pink and stuck on decals that fit a little girl. Then when she outgrew them, back into storage they went. Many years later, when my grandson was born, we took them out of storage again and repainted them brown and again put on boy-type decals. There had been a lot of scraping and sanding and repainting by that time. About the time my grandson was enjoying the little table and chairs, along came my granddaughter – a little more than three years later. By the time she was three years old, my grandson had outgrown the table and chair set. So back to the paint store I went again and selected another shade of pink to use on the little set for my little redheaded granddaughter.

As I write this account of the Christmas table and chairs in the month of March, my grandson is now 16 years old and 6 ft. 7 in. tall and my granddaughter is going to be 13 years old in July, is 5 ft. 6 in. tall, and is taller than I am. So where is the table and chair set? Of course, it is stored in my garage. I had thought we would put it in a garage sale, but my granddaughter is somewhat as sentimental as I am, so we are saving it for my great-grandchildren at her request. They sure made kid furniture sturdy back in the olden days!

One item I received as a Christmas gift was certainly not a girly gift. As stated throughout this book, I usually had boys to play with as a kid, so I learned to play with boy toys. For that Christmas at about age 8, I wanted a football outfit and helmet and a football to go with it. I asked my aunt to buy that for me for my gift from her and my grandmother. She said she would consider it. But when she discussed the potential gift with my mama, my mama securely put her little size four foot down without hesitation! Can't say I blame her, actually. But they both decided it would be O.K. for me to at least have the football and not the entire outfit. So that year one of my favorite toys was that football! I worked at being the kicker on our little neighborhood band of football players, and became proficient beyond my wildest dreams! I got so good at kicking that ball, that I was the only one in the neighborhood that could kick a football clear over the top of the big old sycamore tree across the street. This feat didn't particularly thrill my mama, but the new finally wore off, and we kids advanced on to other activities that interested us.

At Christmas there was also some pretty wearing apparel wrapped up under the tree. I can't remember what all the dresses looked like, but I remember I always received one. And speaking of packages wrapped up for Christmas, I usually knew what my mama and daddy were going to give me, because I knew where they hid them – in the top of the linen closet in the bathroom. Then they began wrapping them before stashing them away up there. I was a clever kid and learned to carefully unwrap them and re-wrap them, so that nobody knew I had peeked. It was part of being a kid and entertaining myself when my mama made a trip by herself to the grocery store. Just kidding around before Christmas.

Two presents that I always received every year at Christmas were a box of chocolate covered cherries and a Nancy Drew mystery book. Of course, since my aunt was a schoolteacher, you can guess who gave me the book. My mama didn't open up the nice living room except on special occasions, and Christmas was one of them. We always had a large tree in front of our big window in the living room, and it was always a real tree. I don't think they even had artificial trees back then. At least not for our homes. It smelled so good in that room. When it was our turn to have everyone in the family over for Christmas dinner, all the adults usually sat around in the big kitchen and talked and drank coffee and cleaned up the after dinner mess. However, I just loved to go into the spice-smelling living room with my box of candy and my book and sprawl out on the couch and read about the latest adventures of Nancy Drew. I literally escaped from the world into those books. God bless my aunt and my mama and daddy for encouraging me to read and get lost in those books and take trips to everywhere and enjoy the adventures of the characters in all those books they provided for me. During the year we made many trips to the library to check out books, but at Christmas I always was gifted with my very own book.

There was one item that I wanted just about more than anything else as a Christmas gift. It was a particular doll. That doll was about 18 inches tall and dressed in full ice skating costume. It even had silver blades on the skates. The dress was blue velvet with a white fluffy furry collar. The skate shoes were brilliant white. The doll was blonde, with long hair and a cap on the head to match the dress, including a white furry border around the doll's face. What a gorgeous doll! Needless to say, that doll was the thing most prominent on display in the toy department of a store downtown. Also, needless to say, it was the most expensive thing in the toy department! As I recall, my mama said it cost $35.00. Today, that would be a drop in the bucket for a toy for a small child. But back in the depression days when I was a child, it was a house payment! I guess it could be compared to giving a 5-year-old child a $600.00 I-Pad or an updated computer! Obviously, the store wasn't really interested in selling that doll, because it was still on display after Christmas, and apparently not on sale, since I was never presented it as a gift. My mama and daddy gave me just about everything I asked for at Christmas, and I know now that they made sacrifices to do that back then. But that doll was absolutely out of each for us financially.

Why did I want that doll so badly, other than the fact that it was beautiful? It was a replica of the 1932 Winter Olympics skating medalist and later skating movie star, Sonja Heinie. Now you understand, and now you know where my parents got my name. That is the year I was born.

If anyone owns that doll now, could I please buy it? It's the only Christmas gift I wanted that I never received – other than the football uniform, that is!

What a Christmas!

Please take a look at the pictures on the next page. Christmas never looked so good. Here is some information about the items in the photo:

My parents must have saved a few dollars all year to be able to provide such a great array of gifts for me. During the 1930s, this kind of Christmas was really spectacular. I want you to notice a couple of things in this picture. All these years, (74 of them since this photo was taken) I have saved the little table and chairs where I am having tea with my doll. It was a cream color when I had it. My son used it many years later and we painted it brown. Then when my daughter came along, we painted it pink and she used it. Much later, when I had a grandson, he played on it at my house and it was painted brown again. A few years after that when my granddaughter came along, we painted it pink again and she used it for several years at my house. Everyone is too old and too large for it now, so it is stored in my garage. I asked my granddaughter if I should put it in a garage sale, and she asked me to save it for her children one day. I wonder what color she will paint it.

That tricycle looks to be just the right size and I loved it. And look at all those other gifts under the tree for the rest of the family. The tree looks a bit scraggly, but it was a real live tree that the whole family had decorated. I still have one of the little Santa Claus ornaments from it.

The other little table in the second photo is one that had a cork-type top where I hammered little pieces with little tacks, to make pretty pictures and other things from imagination. I must have beaten it to death, because it didn't last these many years.

Take a look to the right, behind me in the large photo. For those of you who do not remember, that is an old radio. I wish I still had it. What a classic! The table it sits on is called a "radio table", and I do have it, also, after all these years. It is still beautiful, and so full of memories that I can't part with it. (I also have one of the tiebacks from those drapes. It is stored in an old trunk in my garage. It is wine colored, braided, and has a tassel, just like others of that era.) Yes, I know, my nickname should be "pack rat". But there are some things you just can't part with!

What a wonderful Christmas that was. I know it is impossible to go back in time, but I would sure like to relive that day!

Christmases Past

Kitchen Appliances – Toy and Real

The toy stove:

When I was 4-1/2 years old I was considered to be old enough to know how to handle a toy electric oven. It didn't do much, but I enjoyed "baking" those sweet treats using that very hot little light bulb. I think the person who invented those little ovens was really smart, since they are still popular with little girls many years later. My daddy devised a stand for my toy stove to sit on away from furniture and next to an electrical wall outlet. I had a short-legged stool that I sat on beside my little stove, while I played Betty Crocker. (If you don't know who that was, ask your grandmother.) My stove also cooked food on a small burner on top as well as baking tiny muffins with that little light bulb. My favorite culinary specialty on the top burner was a small amount of scrambled eggs. How good that was with a few of those thimble size muffins!

The real stove:

While I labored over my warm toy stove, my mama made some really delicious stuff on our kitchen stove. I'll describe it to you. My mama's stove was a "Detroit Jewel", I think those were the most classic looking stoves ever made. They had four gas burners on the cook top, with a small overhanging shelf attached to the top of the back of the stove. It held a few salt, pepper and other seasoning jars and cans. To the right of the cook top was the tall oven with a separate broiler below it. It was sort of a pale grayish-green color, as I recall, with chrome and black handles and accents. It stood on legs several feed off the kitchen floor, making it easier to clean under the whole stove. Both the oven and broiler were at about waist height with separate doors – no stooping over there to remove some hot pan. I wonder why they don't make stoves like that anymore. So much easier to remove food from the oven or broiler. And have you pulled out your stove lately and looked at what has collected under it over the past year or two? The floor under that old stove was swept and cleaned daily very easily. Printed on that old stove were the words "Detroit Jewel – They Bake Better". I wish I had that old stove now! It lasted throughout my whole childhood.

The electric refrigerator in our kitchen, when I was very small, was one of those with that big round thing on top to house the motor unit that kept them cold and running. At least I think that was what it was for. It also prevented putting stuff on top of the refrigerator to store it. We were fortunate enough to have an electric refrigerator, because in those days some folks still had "iceboxes". They did not have enough money to purchase an electric refrigerator. "Iceboxes" were large wooden boxes, smaller than our refrigerator, lined with insulating metal around the inside walls, and a similar space attached below to hold a block of ice used to keep food fresh in the top box. They were petty bulky and did not have much room inside to hold food. Needless to say, the ice melted, so the iceboxes had to be refilled very often, sometimes daily. The ice melted and ran into a pan below the icebox. This pan was dumped regularly into the sink or outside onto the flowerbeds or lawn. The iceman came by the neighborhood daily to refill the iceboxes. The ice blocks were carried in the back of the iceman's truck and covered with a heavy tarp to prevent rapid melting. The iceman cut or sawed off the size of ice to fit the icebox it would go into. We neighborhood kids would watch him cut the proper unit for the boxes. After the man had the size he needed, he lifted the block with very large tongs, which had sharp ends that stuck into the ice. The man had a thick leather cover thrown over one shoulder and he hoisted the block of ice, secured by the tongs, onto that cover and began his walk to the house to put the ice into the icebox and collect his fee. This took a few minutes. There was also an ice pick stuck into a block of the ice in the truck bed. When the man was out of sight inside of someone's house, we neighborhood kids would use that pick and sneak chips off of the ice block. We then jammed the pick back into one of the blocks and ran off to some shady spot to hide and enjoy our pilfered ice treats. We didn't consider it thievery. It was hot in the summer and we were just kidding around and cooling off. I am sure glad they have even improved the refrigerators of today. In my current refrigerator, at the touch of a button, those ice chips just fall right into your glass from a slot in the door! I am also glad our refrigerators today hold more food – and have freezers! No ice cream in our first fridge. Ice cream was made in a hand-cranked appliance and eaten right then or it just melted. But I don't care what the advertisements say, it just tasted better done that way. No matter what improvements they have made, they could never improve on hand-cranked ice cream or ice chips sneaked from the back of he iceman's truck!

That's about it for kitchen appliances. Dishwashers were humans back then. Coffee was usually boiled in a pot on the stove. Things took longer to prepare with the absence of microwaves, but it made you hungrier smelling it cooking for a longer time. Hand held beaters were used to mix cake batter, not fancy electric mixers. After meals, when it was time to scrape food from plates, it was dumped into the garbage can, not a current-day sink disposer. Or maybe folks slid the food scraps into the dog's bowl – instead of opening a can to feed their pet. The garbage can was not under the kitchen counter in the form of a modern trash compactor. It sat outside with a lid on it. If something burned on the stove, a door was opened and you fanned your apron to get the smoke out of the kitchen, in the absence of a vent hood over the stove. Actually, all the cooking was done inside the house in our neighborhood, due to the lack of the invention of fancy outdoor grills. My, my, my, haven't we come a long way with all our elegant, timesaving appliances? Shoot…they took all the fun out of it!

The Laundry

During the Great Depression, haute couture just wasn't something our neighborhood folks were really into. Depression days made money too scarce to be able to spend it on designer clothing. Much of a family's clothing was made at home rather than being purchased at a department store. We were all sort of in the same hard times situation in the early 30s, so "ordinary" folks didn't care much if clothes were homemade. This especially applied to the things we kids wore to play outdoors and get dirty. Wardrobes were rather sparse, also, so our mamas were always washing something daily. Ever see a washboard? Know how to use one? Those were common clothes cleaning implements back in the 30s. Kitchen sinks, washtubs and bathtubs and mamas were the washing machines of that era. After the washing came the starching. No spray cans existed back then. Powered starch was mixed with water and the clothes needing to look "starched" were dipped into the starch and water mixture and hand wrung to get ready for the drying process. Later came washing machines that had to be drained by hose outside but not during my early childhood, and we never had one. Those washing machines also had "wringers" – two rubber rollers that pressed together and rolled the clothes through them as you turned the handle. First class stuff way back then – that is if a family could afford one. The "dryer" wasn't plugged into a wall socket. Drying clothes consisted of pinning hem on a clothesline with a couple of wooden clothespins. I have previously described the clothesline setup in detail, and since clothespins still exist, I don't need to explain them here. However, there were no colorful plastic clothespins back then. The sun and breeze dried the clothes, not an electric machine. This was just fine in summertime, but hard to achieve during wet weather. It is uncomfortable to hang wet clothes in very cold weather. The wet clothes were piled into a laundry basket (still not plastic) and toted out to the clothesline. Pretty heavy work sometimes, especially when the basket contained sheets as well as clothing. Don't tell me our mamas didn't work outside our homes!

There were no wash'n'wear clothes in those days; except for underwear and maybe flannel sleepwear and clothes made out of a material they called "seersucker". After our mamas brought the dried clothes back into the house, they got out their ironing boards and began to dampen the clothes, press and smooth out our starched rough-dried clothes to make them more presentable.

Ah, the good old days! Other than hanging clothes on the clothesline, no wonder our mamas didn't work outside the home. They didn't have time!

Dog – Cat – Rabbit

In my early years on Wilton St., I was fortunate to have had three cute pets. They didn't stick around long, but that wasn't my fault. I loved them all. We never actually purchased a pet. Apparently, pet stores were not profitable during the Great Depression.

First there was the puppy. Since there was no leash law in those days, this puppy appeared out of nowhere on our doorstep one day. It just happened to be the week of my birthday. I was so happy that this precious little creature had chosen me! (The picture says it all.) However, his stay at our house was short-lived, also due to the no leash law, and after a few days he wandered off when no one was looking, never to be seen again. Just disappeared one day. As an adult, thinking back on this episode in my young life, I have great suspicion that the puppy didn't move from our house by himself. He was quite active, required a lot of cleaning up after him, chewed on anything available, and did a lot of whining at night, even though my mama put a ticking clock in his bed when it was time for us to have lights out and sleep – or tried to. Apparently he had not heard the old ticking-clock-in-the-dog-bed remedy for whining puppies. He whined anyway. He was so cute and I hate to think that he just didn't like our family. I hope he found a good home somewhere else. I still kind of wonder how he disappeared completely from the neighborhood after a few days. Even if my parents found a new home for him, I hope it was a good one. I guess I will never know. Neither of them ever admitted it.

I don't remember how we acquired the beautiful, full grown white Persian cat with the blue-green eyes that lived at our house on Wilton Street for a while. I think someone gave it to us, but I can't for the life of me remember who. I do remember why it left us, however. The cat's name was Snowball, which was appropriate for her color and fluffiness. She was a lap-kitty that would let you hold her and stroke her back from head to tail, all the while shedding a lot of hair on your clothes. The time I remember most vividly about this feline was the time she ran away from me to hide under my parents' bed. Undoubtedly I had stroked her a little too hard or for a little too long, and she felt it necessary to escape from an overzealous kid. Snowball somehow became entangled under the bed in the underside of the bedsprings. At first she meowed, then she howled and then began to screech very loudly. After yelling for my mama and daddy, I peeked under the bed and the cat spat and hissed at me, so I backed out very quickly. My daddy was already in the room by that time, with my mama close behind. My daddy dove under the bed and began trying to untangle Snowball from the bedsprings. A lot of loud conversation from my daddy followed! I had never heard him use those words before. That cat had used her claws on him unmercifully as he tried to free her. He finally succeeded, and she hightailed it to the back door, where I ran to let her out. She was missing a few tufts of hair, but seemed to be all right otherwise. She just wanted to escape. My daddy, on the other hand, did not fare so well. When I returned to the bedroom, my parents had gone into the bathroom where my mama was in the process of cleaning and medicating the wounds inflicted to my daddy's hands and arms by the cat. His hands were scratched and bleeding on the back and palms and there were long scratches on his arms. What a horrible sight that was! My mama washed them with soap and water first. What made it even worse was his howl when my mama poured alcohol over the wounds to "disinfect" them. I guess alcohol was "it" in those days for disinfecting. My daddy was hopping around like a monkey and yelling "Ouch, ouch, ouch!" I just stood there frozen, watching my mama torture my daddy, and feeling glad that it wasn't me. He said later he didn't know which was worse, the cat scratches or the alcohol burning them. I really felt sorry for him. Apparently he did, too, since a few days later Snowball "disappeared" from our house and neighborhood as magically as the puppy had before her. There was no explanation. I just figured it out by myself. I can't say I blamed him. Anyway, I wasn't a big fan of that cat after that episode. I sure didn't want my hands to be in that shape!

Later, my parents must have felt I needed another pet. This time, a less violent pet for me. They allowed me to have a white bunny rabbit as a replacement. You just can't get less violent than that! One of our neighbors, who lived one street over from our house raised rabbits. He had a lot of little "hutches" behind his house, and occasionally I would wander over there to see them. I became enthralled with a beautiful white bunny with pink-rimmed eyes that lived in one of the pens. I was allowed to stroke and pet it and it seemed to love being held and petted. It didn't have a habit of biting, as many rabbits seem to do when pinned up. One day I asked the owner if he would sell me the rabbit to keep as a pet, if my mama and daddy said I could have it. I told him how the cat had left and he seemed to sympathize with me. He said he would tell my mama that I wanted the rabbit, so we went to my house to ask her. She was a bit skeptical about having a rabbit around the house, especially after all the cleanup behind the puppy, but she and the neighbor made a deal. I could take the rabbit out to play with it at my house everyday if I wanted to do so, but take it back to my neighbor's house to be fed and put back into its pen at night. I also had to stay and help feed it when I brought it back to its pen. There was a small amount of money that changed hands, also, to help pay for the food. What a great deal cooked up by my mama, and what a nice man to allow it. I could have a pet to enjoy; while at the same time have responsibility to care for it, even though not at my house. Sometimes adults can be really smart, can't they? They even helped me name it – "Hoppy", after one of my favorite western movie stars of that era - "Hopalong" Cassidy.

But this pet ownership project was also to be short-lived, and even more tragically. After a few days of going to get the rabbit and bringing it home to play, I decided it needed a "leash" so that we could take walks without an escape. I devised a small collar and leash from a long piece of string that my mama braided for me. After putting it on Hoppy, I took the bunny out to the sidewalk for a walk – or hop- happy kid, pretty bunny, good fun for both.

After a few times during the week of "walking" my bunny back and forth on the sidewalk and in the yard in front of my house, one of the more mischievous, and sometimes mean, little boys in the neighborhood began to take notice. He wasn't someone I usually played with and I didn't want him messing with my rabbit. I think he was a little jealous. I didn't really give him a reason, because he lived at the other end of the street, and I was playing with my bunny in front of my own house. But here he came one day, armed with a short slender metal pole. He insisted on prodding the rabbit along with it, and when I protested and told him to leave the rabbit alone, he whacked my bunny across the back and did a hit-and-run escape back to his end of the street. Poor little bunny, the blow broke his back.

Even though I ran quickly to get my mama and she went quickly with him to our neighbor to be treated, he did not survive. I was heartbroken! My neighbor went to have a long talk with the bad boy's parents. My mama was pretty mad, too, and needless to say, she never allowed that boy to play in our yard again!

It was years later that I realized why the neighbor was raising rabbits. It was depression time and lots of folks thought rabbit stew was a good meal. I guess it was inevitable to lose that rabbit one way or another. We didn't have any more pets for a while after that.

Happy Is The Child Who Has A Pet

Oh the joys of having a warm, snuggly pet to love - - even for a short time. Sorry, there is no photo of the cat. She left too quickly. I doubt my daddy wanted her picture anyway, after what she did to him.

Aside from the joy displayed on my face, the best thing about this photo is the evidence that I had a case of the "droopy drawers". Wouldn't take a million for that one!

The Bonnet

Playing outside in the summer sun was the primary activity for me and my neighborhood pals on Wilton St. It didn't matter what the game was, or how warm it was, we needed to be outside running free. One day when some of us were playing hopscotch on the sidewalk in front of one of the houses across the street from my aunt's house, she yelled at me to come to her house. I did and she told me to play in the shade a while, because she could see the heat waves rising from my head. I don't think I have ever seen that phenomenon before in my life, but she insisted she could see it. So, we retreated to the shade under a tree for a little while. I asked my mother about that later, and she didn't admit to ever seeing anything like heat waves emanating from the top of my head. She just laughed.

I didn't hear anything more about rising heat waves for a few days, and then it happened. The Bonnet! In case you are not familiar with that piece of headgear, a bonnet was usually made of a piece of light weight cotton material that often had a printed pattern of some kind, such as flowers. It was gathered up to make it poufy on top, to allow air to circulate around the top of the head. There was a small bill, made of the same material, attached to the front to shade the eyes. The bonnet had a thin string, also made of the same material, attached to either side and tied under the wearer's chin. That is what mine looked like. Get the picture? Think "granny".

My aunt and grandmother were big on bonnets. In fact, my grandmother made her bonnets and wore them outside in her backyard feeding her chickens or while planting something in her garden when the sun was high in the sky. We little kids made our own breezes running around the neighborhood, but my aunt continued to swear she could see those heat waves rising from my head. Therefore, my grandmother made me a bonnet. Apparently my mama had no say in this two-against-one argument and accepted the bonnet from her mother and used it to envelope my little head. It was probably the only way she knew to end the conversation about heat waves, because she had said to me previously, after one of the discussion between my aunt and grandmother, that she didn't see anything at all rising from my head except my hair. I really didn't want to wear that old lady bonnet, but it was the shortest route to ending the discussion, so I put it on and prepared myself for the jeers of my playmates the next time I went outdoors into the summer sun.

I must have set a fashion trend with that bonnet, because the only little girl in the neighborhood, at that time, wanted one just like it. So my grandmother made her a bonnet. We didn't wear them everyday or even all day – just in the mid-day heat outside. My little playmate actually loved her new hat, but I wore mine to appease my aunt and grandmother. I hated that bonnet! My head would sweat and my hair had to be washed more often, which made my mama not so enthusiastic about the bonnet either.

Many years later, when my grandson was in a daycare, I went there three days a week to read to the little four year olds. I wore a bonnet and long skirt and apron, and they called the reading time a "Story time with Granny". The little girls loved the costume, especially the bonnet. Go figure!

My Daddy's Lap

Every Sunday afternoon after lunch, from the time I was a small tot until my skinny legs began to almost reach the floor, I crawled up on my daddy's lap while he read me the Sunday Funnies from the newspaper, told me a Bible story, and told me a story about when he was a little boy growing up on an East Texas farm. When I was too big to sit on his lap, we still had these Sunday sessions while I sat on the floor in front of him and leaned back on his knees. I believe I learned more stories from the Bible while cuddling on his lap than I ever learned in Sunday School. He was somewhat of a Biblical scholar who could make those stories really come alive for me. I especially loved the Joseph and David stories. Later, as a teenager and then as an adult, I passed those stories along to my own children as well as many other children in Sunday School classes and Vacation Bible Schools, and a Special Education Sunday School class which I taught for 30 years. I probably gained a great deal of reading knowledge while watching and listening to the Sunday comics section being read. My mama read to me almost everyday, also, so she was greatly involved in helping me sort out the words on a page. Everyday at naptime we piled up on her bed and she read a couple of small children's books to me before I finally fell asleep. So, my mama was daily involved in my learning to read process. However, my aunt always took credit for my learning to read by the time I was four years old. I must give credit where credit is due. They all helped teach me to read, no doubt about it. What a nice thing to grow up with – my whole family wanting me to learn to read! That weekly reading of the funnies in my daddy's lap was what really put the icing on the cake as far as I was concerned.

Hearing all those wonderful stories my daddy told me about his growing up in the late 1800s and early 1900s in a rural area, I also learned a bit of Texas history from those colorful memories of his own childhood. It is that which gave me the desire to share some of my own early memories in this book for my grandchildren and anyone else who reads my account of kidding around during the Great Depression years. Let me share some of my daddy's stories with you here:

My daddy was pressed into service as a farmer at an early age. Once while he was holding onto the reins walking behind their big old mule pulling the plow and making furrows across their field, he heard his mama ring the dinner bell back at the house. He quickly unhitched the plow from the mule and jumped onto the mule's back to ride back to the house for dinner. That old mule was apparently just too tired after dragging the plow to proceed at a fast enough pace to suit my daddy. My daddy always carried a small pencil and some note paper with him in his pocket, just in case he wanted to jot down some good thought that occurred to him, while following that plow and mule. So, when the mule didn't move rapidly enough, he pulled out his short, sharp pencil and gave him a poke in the flank. Bad idea! He should have known, but he was hot and hungry and in a hurry to get out of the field and the sun and back to the house for lunch before the other brothers and sisters ate up all the food. The result of the flank poking was that the mule bucked him off and bolted in a run to escape the abuse. When this happened, my daddy became tangled in the plow harness that was still attached to the mule and as the mule ran for the barn, my daddy was dragged along, bumping over the plowed furrows, unable to free himself from the harness. By the time they reached the barn and house area, my daddy was knocked out cold! His clothes were torn, he was bruised and bloody and lucky to be alive. His parents came running when they saw what had happened and detached him from the trembling mule and then revived him. One of my daddy's brothers had to take over the plowing chore in that field after lunch. My daddy was cleaned up, patched up, fed and put to bed for a while. Such was life on the farm. And I always thought it was a boring existence until I heard that tale!

One distinction that my daddy's family had in those early 1900s was the fact that the first telephone switchboard in that farming community was in my daddy's parents' house and tended by his mother. He was not allowed to listen in to any of the conversations, so he had a sparse recollection of that episode in his family life. It was just a great and honorable thing to have in one's house. I imagine the small pay for that endeavor helped a farm family's budget in those days, also.

Of course, I heard the stories of my daddy having to walk miles to school carrying his biscuit and ham lunch in an old syrup bucket. I heard the stories of fights with bullies on the way to school and after school, as well as all the other wonderful firsthand and personal stories about growing up on a rural farm.

How I loved Sunday afternoon reading and story time in my daddy's lap and I still love the memory of my daddy's tale telling. I hope my grandchildren, and all the others who read them, will love my being-a-kid stories as well.

Sand Pile Episode

About age four, my mama decided it was time for me to have a sand pile to play in, in our backyard. Therefore, my daddy, who was good at making things happen for me, constructed a large frame with boards. Later, he attached a bottom to it, made of a sheet of tin, and sat the box on the ground in a small alcove behind and next to our house. It was placed there because it was in full sun, but protected from the north wind in winter, making it a year around play place. I don't know why the sudden urge to build a sandbox in the winter occurred to my mama, but according to the picture, it must have been pretty cold. Maybe the idea was to provide a place for me to play in the winter that was actually out of her way in the house, but a place that could actually be seen easily from the kitchen window so that she could keep an eye on me. I have no idea. In the summer, it seemed to be O.K. to run the neighborhood and disappear from her view, but cold weather seemed to be a different story. The picture of me having a good time in my sand pile looks petty happy, but what happened a few days before was not so great!

Before the bottom of the sandbox was attached to the frame, it was necessary for my daddy to put down a layer of a white substance called lime and spread it on the spot where the sandbox would later sit. This was done to kill the grass there and prevent it from growing up through the box and into the play sand. So, he sat the box down on the spot before attaching the bottom to it and spread the layer of lime thickly over the grassy area within the frame. It needed to sit there for a day or so to do its work, so he left it like that. Of course, I was only a kid and didn't know this procedure, and thought he had poured a bit of white sand into the box and spread it around. I did wonder, however, why it was not a deep sandy layer and why it was so white. I guess I thought he would add more later. I was told to leave it alone, but what kid pays attention to that when a new diversion is so close at hand? Especially not a curious little kid like I was.

The next day after my daddy had left for work and I was bundled up in my coat and cap and sent outside to play and ride my tricycle on the sidewalk for a while, I decided to go back behind our house and examine my new sandbox. That white stuff in the box, that I thought was the first layer of sand, looked so fresh and clean, so I decided to stick my little hand into it, scoop up a handful and let it sift through my fingers. Big mistake! The breeze was blowing and it blew a bit of that white powered lime into my face and right into my eyes and up my nose. Boy, oh, boy, did that stuff burn! I immediately dashed through the back door and into the house, crying and screaming for my mama. She quickly discovered what had happened and called our family doctor. He told her to wash out my eyes and mouth with cold water immediately and blow my nose and then put Argerol drops in my eyes and up my nose. At that particular time, it was hard for me to determine which was worse, the problem or the cure. Argerol was a dark, reddish-brown liquid used to help sinus problems, and luckily for me, my mama had some in the medicine cabinet. It also soothed and stopped the burning sensation of a caustic material if a goofy kid managed to get some of that power in eyes and nose areas. The Argerol came in a little bottle with a dropper, which was used to squirt the stuff into my eyes and nose. It had a definite taste and smell to it, and I can even now remember how it both tasted and smelled as it was inserted into my nose. Before the nose squirting, it was dropped into my eyes to prevent them from burning and possibly causing blindness. I didn't mind that as much, however, it was like looking through a thick brown curtain as it entered my eyes. It was scary, so I cried and rubbed my eyes, staining my clothes with drops of the stuff, and causing my mama to drop more of the stuff into my eyes. The ordeal finally came to an end when the burning stopped and the vision was restored in a few minutes by more cold-water washing. Now you all know what to do if this occurs with a child in your care who is nutty enough to play with lime. Well, I didn't know!

That was an awful day! Due to my mama's quick action, however, there was no damage to my eyes. We made the trip to the doctor the next day and he confirmed that, thank goodness. Soon after that episode, my daddy left the house for a while and returned with several bags of play sand. He attached the bottom to the sandbox and poured in the sand on top of it. No more lime visible to attack his little girl. Now it was a safe place to play.

Those were sure some hard lessons for our whole family to learn:

(1) Pay attention to what your parents tell you not to do, and don't do it, (2) Cover potential problems and hide them from the sight of an overly curious child, and (3) Watch what your kids are doing when they are outside – especially if they are overly curious and get too quiet for a few minutes.

Sand Pile Episode

Early Lessons and Kindergarten

Before going to elementary school, I was fortunate to have the experience of attending kindergarten at Williamson Preparatory School. It must have been a good school, since it lasted far past my childhood into the time that I was grown and married. It even stayed at the same location all that time.

Kindergarten was not just an educational experience. It was also a fun time for me as an only child, because there were so many children to bond with. Most of them were also their parents' only child, so we all sort of became siblings. But before kindergarten, there were some early academics taught to me by my aunt. I loved visiting my "Auntie" (as I called her), because she always had some fun things for me to do. This was probably because she was a schoolteacher. She taught first and second grades at a different elementary school than I would attend later. While I was having indoors fun with my aunt, little did I know that, all the while, she was actually teaching me to read, write and count. So, by the time I was four years old, I could read first grade material and had learned to print and count.

When my parents enrolled me in kindergarten, my aunt was back to her teaching job then. In kindergarten, I excelled because I already knew more than what they were teaching. Looking back, I think the only thing new that I learned there was how to count backward from 100 to 1, as well as how to climb on the monkey bars with other children and how to share with them. We missed all that in my early instructions from my aunt. The sharing with others experience was probably the most important lesson we children all learned, especially as an only child. Up until that time I had not had many neighbor children to play with daily. We kindergarten children were the lucky ones, because by that time most daddies probably had jobs and could afford to send a child to a private kindergarten. Folks don't have to worry about that expense today, due to the fact that most public schools now have kindergarten classes. Hooray for progress in education! Another lasting thing about kindergarten was that I met a couple of children there who would later graduate high school with me, even though, in the meantime, we attended different elementary schools.

BO PEEP: One of my fondest memories of kindergarten is of a play – or maybe just a "production" to show off our questionable talents. I was delighted to have the most beautiful costume of anyone. At least I thought it was. Little Bo Peep. It was a blue satin shoe-top length dress with those little "pouches" on the sides like the picture in books. I had a hat upon my little head, also, just like the original Bo Peep. To complete the ensemble, I carried a shepherd's crook staff (also wrapped in blue satin) and I wore new black patent leather shoes. The strange thing about that production is that I can't remember having a sheep, nor can I remember who played a sheep – if there actually was one. I think I was so enthralled by the beautiful costume that I can't remember much else. There were not many such beautiful dresses in our small world back then, because no one could afford them – only in a play. I think the whole theme of the production was nursery rhymes, since I remember one of the girls dressed as a fat yellow and black spider. So glad it wasn't me! I also can't remember who played Miss Muffet. Hmmm…. I guess I really was mentally all wrapped up in that beautiful costume! You can see what nursery rhymes were represented by looking at the photo on the next page.

Kindergarten really was full of good things after all. I wonder how much my parents had to sacrifice to send me there, pay for that beautiful costume, and buy those patent leather shoes. But, then, that was what parents did back then.

Kindergarten – Mother Goose Play

I Learned To Swim At The "YM"

I really did learn to swim at the YMCA. I have a badge to prove it, even though I was a little girl of about five years old and not a man! These days that is not uncommon for kids to learn to swim at the "Y".. However, back in the 1930s the downtown Dallas "Y" was strictly a guy thing. Now, in small surrounding communities and cities there are many YMCA facilities serving both male and female in a variety of activities. Progress marches on with time. But my swim button was very unique back when I was a little girl. And I still don't know why they called it the Young Men's Christian Association, since there sure were a lot of old dudes and Jewish guys that were members at the time I was growing up. However, none of those guys were there when I learned to swim at the "YM"

Since my daddy was an employee of the "Y", my family and a few small friends of mine were allowed to use the facilities on Friday nights after the Health Club closed for the day. On some of these "Family Nights", a few of my neighborhood pals were treated to come with us to use some of the workout equipment, but mainly to use the pool. My daddy taught us all, including my mama, to swim and dive in that pool. He really worked with us until we had all learned to stay afloat and eventually we learned to swim the width and then the length of the pool. After we swam to his satisfaction, we were presented a large badge that said "I leaned to swim at the YM'. I still have my badge. When I wore it as a child, it sometimes was a real conversation piece!

Friday night swim night was pretty tame and simple entertainment compared to today's pool and fitness center activities. Many folks have their own pools these days, but back then nobody in our neighborhood had even thought of having a pool in their backyard. During the Great Depression, luxuries such as a pool were not on the list of things to own. Food, clothes and a place to live, as well as a job to provide those things, trumped such items as pools. I have managed to survive all these years without one, also. A trip to Cancun a few years ago, and a few trips to

Galveston, shows me how far we have come since depression years, as well as how far we will go to have fun in the water. However, I have the luxury of the memory of the splashing fun we kids had learning to swim in the YMCA pool.

I have often wondered if that effort and act of love on my daddy's part, to see that we all learned to swim, managed to stay in the memories of those kids like it did in mine. I guess I will never know.

The Wilton St. "Gang"

Looks like at least two of us were age 5, judging by the loss of a front tooth. Probably the reason my daddy took this overly wide grin photo. What we were wearing, with the exception of someone's little sister, was called "sun suits" and they were probably homemade. Mine was made of corduroy material. Aren't we just the cutest kids you ever saw!

Radios and Radio Programs

Since TV had not been invented yet for home entertainment, we stayed glued to our radios in my childhood days. One of my earliest memories was listening to the old round top radio my family had sitting on our "radio table". I still have that table in my home after all these years. I just wish I could have retrieved the old radio as well.

As a little kid, my favorite radio program was "Little Orphan Annie and Her Dog Sandy". Her father was called Daddy Warbucks, and he was apparently a single parent who had adopted Annie, who was apparently an orphan. Daddy Warbucks was also some sort of government agent who had many adventures in which Orphan Annie became involved in some way. As with all children's programs on the radio, there was always a way for the young audience to become involved, also. The person connected to that Annie program who devised the "decoder rings" was a genius at kiddie involvement. Here is how it worked: You ate all the cereal (or whatever product the advertiser was selling) that you could consume, and when you had enough box tops to send them, they would mail you your prize. In Annie's case, it was a "decoder ring". Then each day that the program was on, at the end of each episode, there was some sort of "cliff hanger", leaving the avid fan wanting more information. In order to be one jump ahead of everyone else, you had to have a "decoder ring". The announcer would say that the following numbers would reveal a clue to what was going to happen in the next episode. He would then slowly call out a string of numbers, so kids could write them down. The top of the ring had both numbers and letters on two levels. After receiving the numbers from the announcer, you then revolved the top tier of the ring to match up the numbers with the letters on the tier below. That gave you the cryptic message about the next episode.

On one occasion that I remember very distinctly, my mama had gone next door to see my aunt for a few minutes and left me at home listening to Annie. She had been gone for only a few minutes when the program ended. I was frantic! I could not find a piece of paper to write down the code numbers as the announcer began calling them out. My daddy had not come home from work yet, so I was on my own without paper. I just collapsed in a shower of tears while the announcer slowly droned on. I should have known my mama would not have let me down. She never did. My aunt also had the radio turned on and my mama wrote down all the numbers for me. She quickly returned home to find me on the floor having a hissy! Needless to say, I recovered my composure immediately when she showed me the decoding numbers. Then she helped me use the ring to get the secret message. Whew! That was a close one. And what a mama!

Other favorite radio programs of mine were: "Let's Pretend", "The Shadow", "The Green Hornet", "One Man's Family", "I Love a Mystery", and "Young Widow Brown"

"Let's Pretend" was a radio program for very young children that aired on Saturday mornings. It was something I always looked forward to on the weekend. It came on with the playing of the song "Country Gardens", followed by the announcer introducing the person responsible for those wonderful programs, Nila Mack. Her name has stuck in my mind all these years and I hope I have spelled it correctly. Does anyone out there remember her? I also remember the announcer's name – Les Tremane – whom I have seen years later on TV. The reason I knew who he was is that I vividly remember his voice. Imagine that! I hope I have spelled his name correctly, also. After introducing Ms. Mack, the announcer came back and announced what we were going to pretend that day, and off we went, deep into our imaginations, right along with the action and colorful characters. The program, through these great actors' voices, presented different children's stories each week. We pretended we went right along with them on their various adventures. There were no visuals, just the audio story of what was happening. The pictures of it came to life in our own minds. Now, don't get me wrong; I love to watch TV programs. But I see the children of the current TV program era just sit and have whatever is on the screen fed into their eyes with no thought of action going on in their imagination. It is a shame that today's kids don't have that advantage of mental pictures painted by their imaginations that were presented to us by our radio programs. Sadly, a lost or dying art for our children and grandchildren. I think they are missing an important part of kidding around – imagination.

"The Shadow" was a mystery program, which always began with the announcer saying, "Who knows what evil lurks in the hearts of men? Only The Shadow knows!" Then the disguised, do-gooding guy known as "The Shadow", went about discovering evil, righting wrongs, and doing good when nobody actually saw him. Thus his name of "The Shadow". Good lesson for kids – do good even when nobody is watching.

"The Green Hornet" was also a crime-fighting guy in disguise with an assistant (or houseboy) by the name of Kato. This crime eliminator rode around in a sharp car, driven by Kato. When he took off and left home to fight the bad guys, you knew it – the car had a very loud muffler! I imagine it was to remind you of a swarm of hornets taking flight.

Another radio mystery favorite when I was a little older was "I Love a Mystery", which began with a squeaking door opening and closing. – as though in some old haunted castle. I can't remember any of the stories, but I do remember the names of the crime and mystery busting characters. They were Jack, Doc and Reggie. I have always wondered where these radio program writers came up with the names of their characters. This program came on at my usual bedtime, so I didn't get to tune in and hear it often. When I did, I usually fell asleep listening to it, which is probably why I can't remember much of the content.

The other programs I mentioned were "soap operas" which I usually listened to with some member of my family.

Frequently, on Sunday afternoons, my daddy and mama would take the family on long drives out on country roads just relaxing and driving along. Some of those drives involved looking for loaded pecan trees to empty, but more often it was just to take a Sunday afternoon drive and chat with my aunt and my grandmother, who usually went with us. Even then, I suppose people needed to get away from city life for a while. At some point, on these long drives, my daddy always turned on the car radio. Yes, we had one – no heating and cooling, but there was indeed a radio in our car. I think he turned on the radio when he had enough of hearing all the women's voices yakking while he drove. Anyway, we all enjoyed the radio programs on our Sunday afternoon drives.

One special program we all loved to listen to was a true "soap opera" called "One Man's Family". Maybe there was some satire there for my daddy sitting in the car with four females. The program was all about the trials and tribulations of this one family. It kept us all quiet, listening and being entertained for a while. I am sure my daddy's motive for turning on the radio was the peace and quiet it brought, however.

Another "soap opera" that my grandmother particularly enjoyed listening to on weekdays at home was "Young Widow Brown". The program related, in a very dramatic way, a young widow's problems while raising her children alone. It was a real hit radio show in those days of stay-at-home mothers and grandmothers. Those gals used to drop what they were doing and grab a cup of coffee and just sit and listen to the radio. I guess much like today's stay at homes watch their "soaps" on TV. Some things never change – just the method of delivery.

Did someone ask why these daytime melodramas were all called "soap operas"? The answer is simple. Those programs, which were aimed at the attention of housewives and grandmothers at home, all advertised some brand of washing powder. We still call them "soaps" today, even though they are advertising many more items to interest women than just washing powder. You just can't top a good nickname. Hooray for the "soaps"!!

My daddy had been interested since he was a boy in putting together a form of radio known as a crystal set. One day, he decided to assemble a little different type of communication system for me. Since he had been a radio operator in the Navy in WWI, he knew Morse Code. He taught it to me through this new toy he devised for me. He took a cigar box and installed the "workings" of this apparatus inside, including a battery and some wires. Then he brought out of his storage space in the garage a telegrapher's key that he had brought back years before when he discharged from the Navy. He connected it on top of the cigar box to the stuff inside, and voila we had a telegraphic communications set. We had lots of fun with it. It made a beeping noise of the dots and dashes of Morse Code when you pressed the key. I would go into another room and peck out the code message, and my daddy would write it down in the next room. Then he would do the same thing with the box, and I had to write down the message. The big Morse Code message we all heard during the WWII days was the V for Victory signal – dot, dot, dot, dash. We all learned that one!

What simple fun I had with my daddy and mama, while I was just kidding around and learning new things at the same time.

I'm An Old Cowhand

I'm an old cowhand…..from the Rio Grande.
But my legs aint bowed….and my cheeks aint tanned.
I'm a cowboy who never saw a cow
Never roped a steer, 'cause I don't know how,
And I sure aint fixin' to start in now.
Yipee-aio-Kyaa

(or something like that)

(Shirt, hat, and chaps bear the named of old time movie cowboys
Hoot Gibson and Buck Jones. Bazooka named for old time comedian
Bob Burns. Kid cowboy is me, and my cheeks are tanned!)

The $10.00 Bike

Times were hard. Budgets were tight.
Kids still needed to own a bike.

Although children of the Great Depression era became accustomed to doing without most luxuries, we all still needed toys. We also learned a lot about sharing of toys, as well as taking good care of them and making them last. I imagine in today's world in this country, there are very few children who have never had a bike or at least access to a shared bike. Today's kids have probably had several of them of different sizes by he time they reach middle school age. Not so during the depression years.

By the time I had reached age five, I had acquired one "Kiddie Kar", which required feet on the ground pushing it along, and a tricycle when I expertly pedaled down the sidewalk. Back then, larger toys like those were only afforded as Christmas presents. I was more fortunate than most kids, also. I rode both vehicles until I was too big for them. I knew by the time I was five years old that I wanted a bike more than anything else in the world! But it was summertime by then – not Christmas. I couldn't wait.

One day, when I was playing with a kid on the next street over from our house, I discovered someone who had a bike for sale. They were moving away from our neighborhood to another state in a few days, and needed to sell the bike quickly. There was a $12.00 price tag on it. That sounds like a garage sale price these days for sure, for a used small tricycle, but during the Depression that price bordered on exorbitant pricing for a used bicycle.

I told the lady who owned the bike that I would run home to ask my mama if we could buy it. After all, my daddy was one of the fortunate people who had a decent job at that time. So I immediately dashed home to start the begging. My mama was pretty shocked when I burst into the house and began my spiel about why I needed that $12.00 bike. She said she would have to discuss it with my daddy. I just couldn't wait for fear it would be sold by the time he returned home from work, so she gave in and called him at work and discussed whether or not the family budget could stand a $12.00 hit before Christmastime. My mama and daddy finally decided that I could have the bike if there was enough money left in the grocery budget to buy it, but he wanted to negotiate the price down to $10.00. Even that was a lot of money in those days. Besides, my mama had told him she had only $10.00 left in her purse. He still agreed to buy the bike for $10.00 and asked her to use her grocery money to buy it if they could agree on the price. I only heard my mama's side of the whole conversation, and stood there stock still after she hung up the phone. Then she turned to me as I held my breath and told me I could have the bike if I could make a deal for the $10.00. I think she was embarrassed to go make the offer, so she handed me the only money from her purse – a $10.00 dollar bill and told me to see what I could negotiate for the bike.

Needless to say, I snatched that bill, kissed and hugged her, and ran as fast as I could make my little bare feet fly back to the lady with the bike. When I turned up there with the cash, that lady couldn't wait to take the money and turn the bike over to me and she quickly pocket our grocery money; now, her grocery money.

That bike was painted blue, which has always been my favorite color. It had skinny racing tires and no frills, but now it was mine! I didn't know how to ride such a large bicycle, but I was sure I could learn, with the help of my mama and daddy. After all, they made a sacrifice for me to own the bike, so I knew they would take plenty of time to make sure I could learn to ride it. Sure enough, they took an afternoon to help me learn to balance that big old bike and maneuver it all over our neighborhood. I could barely reach the pedals, but I was determined to be a proficient five-year-old bike rider. What a wonderful feeling that was to finally go breezing along the street and sidewalk on my own bike! It couldn't have been any better if it had cost a million dollars. I rode that bike for many years, even through another set of tires. It was the only bike I ever owned as a kid and I loved it as much as if it was a brand new one.

I learned later that my parents had planned to buy me a new bike for Christmas the year that I bought the $10.00 bike, but that didn't matter. That used bike meant a lot more to me than a new one. It meant an immediate sacrifice by my parents, and in the process I learned how to "negotiate" – with cash. I also learned that's not something you just kid around with when you are trying to make a deal.

First Grade School House

It never entered my mind that I lived in the "dark ages" when I was five years old, but when I think back to the first grade schoolhouse, it does seem a bit primitive. The white frame building had rooms on the left side and rooms on the right side, with a wide and open, but covered, breezeway between the two sides of the building. The building must have been sitting on some sort of pier and beam foundation, because it was necessary to go up several steps to enter the breezeway and then veer off to the left or right into a room. My first grade room was to the right. When I describe the open connection between rooms as a "breezeway", I mean just that. Although it afforded a shady retreat in hot weather and a shelter from rain since it had a roof, it was a perfect spot for those winter winds to blow through! There was no air conditioning in that school building either – just fans and heaters, like in our homes. I guess all that qualifies it as "primitive".

But as primitive as that building was, the real back woods qualifying structure was found behind the school building. It was a free standing building that was probably at least twenty feet from the school with no covered area or paved walkway between the two buildings. It was called the Girls and Boys Bathrooms. Yes, indeed, it was outside and if you were really needing to "go" you had to hurry right along across the school building breezeway, down the steps and across the yard to do your business. The structure was rectangular in shape with a sign on the left door opening reading "Girls" and on the right the sign read "Boys". These two areas were separated by a common wall between them. There was a separate entrance to each side, however. One of the fun games the boys played in first grade was to chase the girls into the bathroom when we were on the playground. I don't know why – a guy thing, I guess. Maybe they just liked to hear us squeal as we ran for cover in the bathroom.

I was only five years old when I started first grade. Since my aunt and parents had already taught me to read, print and some simple math,

I breezed through kindergarten and was ready for first grade when I was barely five in January. I was actually put a grade ahead at mid-term, rather than waiting until the next regular school year to enroll in first grade. This was permissible in those days; however, my parents had to pay a fee for me to attend public school at the age of five. Back then I didn't know I was smart. I just wanted to go to school! Now I wonder at the judgment or wisdom of early registration. My intent in writing this chapter is not to tell of my early entrance into school. It is actually to paint the reader a picture of how our school buildings were so primitive. That's the only word I can think of to describe them. Nevertheless, we sure were taught all the basics very well by those early teachers, allowing us little upstarts of that era to learn to study properly and try to achieve greatness and make something of ourselves. Quite a challenge during the depression. And those teachers did that in the little white frame schoolhouse with the outdoor restrooms and didn't seem to let the "primitive" conditions affect their ability to cram knowledge into our little heads. Three cheers for the teachers of that day!

Apparently the teachers' hard work, together with our desire to learn and progress, was successful. Just think of all the inventions, updates of almost everything, wealth, winning wars with unimaginable weapons, putting men on the moon, medical advances, television, computers we can hold in one hand, cell phones, I-pods, and you-name-it innovations and progress that the kids growing up when I did have helped to accomplished. And it all started with all of us being relatively poor, some of us going to school in primitive schoolhouses, knowing we had to study and learn, then encouraging our children to be achievers, keeping our religious beliefs alive and passing them on, and always keeping our sense of humor in tact. Today the buildings where our grandchildren and great grandchildren go to study, using the most top-notch equipment ever devised, are magnificent brick and stone structures featuring many windows and indoor modern plumbing. Some even have elevators to accommodate the handicapped students. Think back what has been accomplished since I was born in 1932! Amazing and mind-boggling. But we children of the Great Depression era helped it all to happen despite the adversity around us at times. Shows you how special we were, and we managed to help accomplish all these wonders starting out just kidding around in little frame schoolhouses. Three cheers for our generation, also!

Shopping Trips and Streetcars

Since my mama never learned to drive a car, we rode the streetcar during the day to go shopping in downtown Dallas. My daddy usually took the car to work. In order to board the electric rail streetcar, with its overhead lines connected to the electrical wires, you needed a "token". These were thin dime-size coins with slits punched out around the middle, so as not to confuse them with actual dimes. I can't remember how much these tokens cost, since I never purchased them myself, but they were much cheaper than gasoline, even though gasoline was relatively inexpensive, especially as compared to prices in the past 50 years. My mama carried a little pocket size token holder that held several tokens and dispensed one at a time as they popped up to the top by way of a small spring like mechanism. I still have one of those dispensers and one token from the past.

We lived in the Oak Cliff section of Dallas, so it was necessary to rock along in the streetcars and over the long bridges from where we lived into the west edge of downtown Dallas. This was after we had walked the six blocks from home to the streetcar line to board the streetcar in the first place. When we reached our downtown Dallas destination, we got off and walked some more from what was at the time Sanger Brothers Department Store all the way through town to the eastern part to end our shopping at Titche-Goettinger Department Store. (Back then we called them Sangers and Titches.)

On the way, and in between these two stores, we shopped at other small stores and boutiques such as A. Harris, Lerner's and Sam Deistebach (can't remember the exact spelling) and W.T. Grant Variety Store. Obviously, judging from the names, the town was full of good Jewish merchants. Since we had very limited funds, we mostly "shopped" instead of spending. We only looked at the window displays of the Neiman-Marcus department store and didn't spend any time shopping inside. It was way higher than our modest budget! My mama had a seamstress that made many of our clothes. That lady would also look at the clothes on display in the windows of some of these stores, including Neiman Marcus, and then make patterns of the styles to make for us. My mama would purchase the fabric, thread, buttons and any other decorative items needed, then the seamstress would make the clothes for us. She was a very inexpensive seamstress and this helped our budget and allowed me to be well dressed as a child in spite of the Great Depression. Not only didn't my mama learn to drive a car, she also didn't learn to sew; maybe a few repairs, but no dressmaking. We had a portable Singer sewing machine, but it mostly just sat out in the hall. It wasn't used very often. I still have that old Singer. I don't use it either! It is just a beautiful antique.

Trips to our dressmaker's home where she did her fantastic sewing were also via streetcar, which went directly in front of her house. We brought her all the goods to make the clothes and she cut patterns for us to match what she had seen in the various store displays. After that we waited a few days and she would call and tell my mama that we were ready for a fitting. This meant that she would "pin" patterns on us, or maybe pin some fabric on us, depending on the progress of the sewing job. Always afterward my mama and the seamstress lady had a visit and I played with her children. Sometimes we ate a light lunch with them. During these visits they always had jokes to share with each other. I guess keeping morale up in those days was something everyone did for each other. They were very good friends and those were some fun visits – except for the part where I had to stand perfectly still for the "pinning"

Now, back to the streetcars. When I was small, not yet six years old, after walking the six blocks to the end of the streetcar line nearest our home, it was sometimes necessary to wait for a while until the next car came. You never knew for certain when that would be even though they had some sort of schedule. There was a little convenience type store on the corner across from the end of the streetcar line and sometimes we waited there on the bench outside. Then, when the car arrived, the driver (whom we all referred to as the conductor) would allow us to board it, but then we sat and waited a little longer while the conductor went to the convenience store and bought a snack or drink or maybe use the bathroom, since there was no restroom on the streetcars. When he returned it was necessary for him to re-position the overhead electrical lines in the opposite direction from which he came. Let me mention here that there was no heat or air conditioning on those streetcars, so we either dressed warmly in winter and kept the windows closed or dressed lightly in summer and opened the windows to let the air flow as we rode along – much like we were required to do in our automobiles. How times have changed and made public transportation much more comfortable. Oh, yes, there were no padded seats either, just wooden benches which each accommodated two persons. Not too comfortable as the streetcar bumped and swayed along its winding its way through the neighborhoods and then across the "viaduct" (long bridge) into the downtown Dallas area. If the streetcar was full of people, it was necessary to stand in the aisle clinging to an overhead leather looped strap attached to a bar. Quite a balancing act at times as the car swayed around some corners. The conductor stopped at just about every corner sometimes to let passengers' board or exit, so it took quite a while to reach our downtown destination. Notice that any reference to the conductor was "he". That is because back then there was no female streetcar conductor. The conductors also seemed to be older men, probably due to the fact that so many men were in the military services about that time. These conductors wore uniforms similar to the ones worn by the men who collected tickets on trains. But when you boarded a streetcar, you paid the fare right then. There was a pole next to the conductor's seat up front which had a box connected to it where you dropped in your coins or tokens. It whirred and did something that I, as a little kid, never did figure out and then it dropped the coins to the bottom of the box. As the box filled, the conductor had a bag into which the coins were emptied and later turned into the streetcar "barn" along the way or at the end of his shift.

Another of the conductor's duties was to change the signs from the front to the back of the car when he reached the end of the line. As a little kid, I could never understand why the black people were required to sit in the assigned seats in the back of the streetcars; this was designated by a movable sign that hung on the wall over the seats. The sign read "Colored" and all black people had to sit behind that sign. The sign was sometimes moved back by passengers, as well as the conductor, as the car filled with riders who were not "colored". When the car was full, everyone hung on the aforementioned straps – black people to the back, white people to the front. Thank goodness this didn't happen frequently.

I asked my mama why black people had to sit in the back of the streetcars and why they had to only drink from water fountains marked "Colored", and why they couldn't use the same restrooms as we white folks used. She simply said that it was because they were black and that it was the law. I said to her on more than one occasion that I could not understand such a law. She assured me that she couldn't understand it either. When my mama was a small child living in Louisiana her family had black workers who lived in small houses at the back of their property, and one of her daily playmates was a child of one of those workers. My mama said they played with her dolls under the raised porch of their big house where it was shady and cool. She said her family always saw to it their workers had a house to live in, plenty of food and clothing and other necessities and always treated them well. My mama said her family often sat on their back porch in the evening after dinner, listening to their workers singing as they sat outside around their own little houses. I suppose that is why she had a different point of view than the lawmakers who erected the "Colored" and "White Only" signs all over the place. Just goes to show that sometimes it's all in how a person is raised, I guess. And haven't we come a long way along a rocky road to where we are now!

Downtown Eateries We Enjoyed

On many shopping excursions into downtown Dallas with my mama, we would eat at either Dunton's Cafeteria or at Cabell's.

Dunton's was a large cafeteria in the middle of downtown. It had large glass front windows and many tables looking out these windows. There were also several large chandeliers overhead to light the area. When you entered the front door, you continued down the wide center aisle, with dining tables on either side. That main aisle led to the back of the restaurant in a space under an overhanging balcony where the cafeteria line began. This was not a very large area and it was in a curved or horseshoe shape. But there was plenty of delicious food! I always ordered the mashed potatoes and brown gravy, along with their large and very tasty cone-shaped salmon croquettes with lots of tarter sauce on the side. My dessert was always half a cantaloupe, which was hollowed out and filled with a large scoop of ice cream inserted in the hollow. I can still recall how good all of that tasted, even though my mama's home cooking was equally as delicious. When you finished making the curve and ordering your food, you paid at the cash register at the end of the line. Then off you went to find a table. That cafeteria also had a wide stairway at the back of the large eating area that led to another eating area upstairs on a balcony. It was a little difficult to navigate those stairs while carrying your tray of food, but sometimes there was a cafeteria worker who helped a lady and/or small child by carrying the tray up to the balcony. Sure hard to find that kind of assistance these days most places. Something else hard to find these days is a large cloth napkin with a full array of silver eating utensils wrapped inside. Just imagine a cafeteria having that already on the tables ready for your use! There were not any little packets of seasonings either. There were nice clear glass salt and pepper dispensers and several other seasonings on every table. And if you needed something else, there was a lady who would fetch it for you and she didn't even expect a tip. Even though my mama was a wonderful cook, there was something really special about eating at Dunton's.

Sometimes we ate at Cabell's. This small café had a narrow storefront and interior area. Most of the eating area was upstairs which was reached by way of a narrow stairway. You ordered from a variety of sandwiches, but the most delicious and most popular was their thinly sliced and piled high roast beef on a hoagie poppy seed bun with a side of clear gravy in which you dipped the sandwich before biting into it. What do we call it? A "French Dip", I believe. Not fancy eating, but totally delicious. The Cabbell family owned a dairy – Cabbell's Dairy, so to wash down their sandwiches, we always had a small carton of their milk. One member of that family – Earl Cabbell – was at one time the Mayor of Dallas. I sure wish they still had Cabbell shops today, and farmed them out as franchises. I loved those roast beef sandwiches! Oh, yes, we do have something similar today, I think, known as Arby's. Maybe that is where they got the idea – from those 1930s Cabbell's thin sliced roast beef sandwiches. Yeah, and I have to admit, they are both delicious!

My daddy and my grandmother occasionally went together to eat raw oysters at a downtown oyster bar. I say those two went together, because nobody else in my family would even give a thought to eating a raw oyster, and we didn't want to watch them do it! I still cannot understand why people want to eat them. I guess it is a learned behavior that I never studied for, and at my current age I have no plans to do so.

Another small place where we enjoyed occasionally on our downtown trips was Shoemaker's Bar-B-Q. Now, that's something I can still latch onto and really down a lot of it with pleasure. Maybe the love of good barbeque is part of a Texan's genes. This dispenser of scrumptious meat was also housed in a narrow facility, but with no balcony. It was located on the ground floor of the old Mercantile Bank building – the one with the big clock on the top, across the street from Neiman-Marcus. Other than the delicious bar-b-q and the very odor of it, the real charm of this hole-in-the-wall eating-place was the sawdust on the floor! If you don't know, sawdust was placed there to absorb the grease from the meat dropped on the floor. I think it was also about the rustic atmosphere the sawdust produced. Along both sidewalls were school-type armchair desks lined up ready for folks to sit and savor their barbeque sandwiches. The order counter was at the back, so you got to swirl your way through the sawdust to get to it. You both ordered and paid for your food there. They had both ham and beef sandwiches on big round buns and a variety of bottled drinks. I always ordered the chopped beef sandwich – easy to eat – and a small grape soda called "Grapette" The name fit the size of the small bottle, which was easy for a small child to hold because it was not very big around. Small though it was, it was sure a tasty grape drink! It was so good with the barbeque. (Are you hungry yet?) You could just eat like a kid there since you never had to worry about any of that meat or grease or sauce dripping on the floor. The sawdust took care of that. However, sometimes when we were exiting the place, I had to go to the curb to empty the sawdust from my sandals. I am so sad that place is not there anymore. I would still enjoy acting like a kid, shuffling my way through that sawdust to get to my delicious sandwich. No place around like that anymore for kids to shuffle through and not worry about the cleanup if a piece of their sandwich fell to the floor. At least I haven't found one lately. What a shame.

After the Shopping Trips – Meeting My Daddy

In the summertime, when I was not in school, after my mama and I went to downtown Dallas on some of our shopping trips, we frequently met my daddy after he got off from work. On these summer trips we usually went to Dallas after eating lunch at home and when we met my daddy we ate at Dunton's Cafeteria most of the time. After eating our evening meal we would take in a movie. There were two nice theaters downtown – the Palace and the Majestic. They were both on Elm Street a few blocks apart and not far from the restaurant. It wasn't worth waiting for a streetcar to take us a few blocks, so we usually walked to one of the movies. Back then many people were strolling down the three main streets of downtown Dallas either just window-shopping or headed for a movie. Maybe folks were slimmer back then because we walked more to wherever we were going.

So off we strolled to the movie doing our own window shopping. No stores were open late, so that is all we could do and not spend money going in and out of them. These days it doesn't seem to be the safest environment to do that at night. Back then no one bothered us or attempted to rob us. What a different world we live in today!

Both theaters were beautiful, elegant, and a far cry from our neighborhood movie house, which we referred to as "The Bloody Bucket" because they showed so many cowboy and gangster shoot-em-ups in our small neighborhood theater. The downtown theaters were carpeted and had up-to-date décor, even in the restrooms. They had balconies and soft plushy seats throughout. They also had well stocked candies of the era and popcorn counters in the lobby. There were no hotdogs or nachos or other plates of food at the candy counters then. There were also no seating areas to hang out in and eat. These snack bars were not at all the length of those in today's theaters, and they had nothing like the inventory of things to eat and drink that today's theaters have. In fact they were very small and inadequate by today's standards, but they were wonderful to us. We were fortunate that my daddy had a job and could take us out to dinner and a movie once in a while during the years of the Great Depression. More than that wasn't expected. It kept folks going. I didn't even realize we were poor!

I must describe the back-in-the-day Majestic Theater to you. And by the way, this theater is still active in downtown Dallas, but I haven't been there in many years. So I will describe to you how beautiful it looked to me as a kid. The Majestic really lived up to its name back then. After buying a ticket from a lady in a booth next to the sidewalk, you went through double doors and entered the theater on a beautiful red swirly, plush carpet. Overhead was a very large crystal chandelier. Straight ahead was a carpeted wide stairway, which fanned out into the lobby, and then narrowing somewhat as it ascended to the balcony area. I can only remember sitting in the balcony with my parents one time, however. They preferred to sit about two-thirds of the way down on the lower floor. I imagine this was because there were no gigantic screens or surround sound in movie houses back then.

One treat that both major downtown theaters featured occasionally was live entertainment on the stage before or after the movie was shown. It was also imperative to hold onto your ticket stub, because sometimes there was a drawing for prizes and free movie tickets or free snacks from the candy counter and at Christmas tine they even had a special drawing for a bicycle. I can't remember our family ever winning anything. I do remember being there when some kid won a new bike. Lucky kid!

Something else that attracted folks to the downtown Majestic was the live organ music between shows. The organ was on an elevator platform type of lift, which was below floor level at the front and left of the stage area. Movies had "intermissions" so that you could visit the candy counter and also restrooms. During these intermissions, and also after the movie, the organ (with the organist sitting on the bench) rose up to floor level and we all had a "sing-along". The words were shown up on the movie screen with a little bouncing ball over them so you could follow along and sing as the organist played the song. Sound corny? Maybe so, but it really was fun and added to the length of the whole evening's fun and entertainment. Of course after all these live attractions; we got back to the business of watching the movie. There was always a cartoon and usually a "short subject" shown as well as the "coming attractions". Sometimes there were even double features! More for your money in those days could draw a crowd. One thing missing then that we see a lot of today was business advertising on the screen before the movie began. It was either too expensive to do that during the Great Depression time, or else nobody had even thought of it yet.

The actors and actresses in those movies were so glamorous and envied. They lived like kings and queens. Even now, just looking back at their clothes and cars makes you want to own those things! The closest a poor kid back then could get to owning them was through our books of paper dolls. I just loved cutting them out and folding the little tabs at the top of the clothes over their shoulders and pretending to walk them around dressed so elegantly. My two favorite paper dolls were Ronald Reagan and Jane Wyman, who were a couple of glamorous movie stars who were at that time married to each other. Who knew that many years later they wouldn't be married, and he would be the President of the United States! Those were great years kidding around with paper dolls and those were great years for our country later with Reagan as President. It seems these days everyone in Hollywood wants to get into the act – politically, that is – not on the silver screen! My, how times change. Later, Barbie and Ken came along for my daughter to amuse herself, and currently, who knows what's out there for little kids to play with. I am sure it has something to do with electronics or computers. Seems to me my generation had more playthings that promoted family rather than glamour, and things that made us use our imagination rather than our thumbs. Just a sign of the times, I guess. Or maybe I am getting older and more critical.

It was such simple fun being a kid back then. (Sigh) I sometimes yearn for those "good old days" when families did simple fun things together even in hard times. Maybe that is what held all of us poor families together back then…we had to stick together and do our best to enjoy each other and ourselves. There's a lesson in there somewhere for today's families, don't you think?

Eddie & Jimmie

Two of my daddy's brothers were pretty successful in the entertainment business. They took the last name of "Dean". Changing their names in those days was a common practice with entertainers and movie stars. They were Eddie Dean and Jimmie Dean. (No, not the sausage maker Jimmy Dean.) The two brothers sang on a Chicago radio station back in the 1930s. I still have an old "yearbook" of that station's personalities, with both brothers' pictures in it. They also sang on a popular program of that era, The National Barndance. Uncle Jimmie had an exceptionally fine tenor voice, and Uncle Eddie had a really smooth and beautiful baritone voice. Jimmie Dean went on to sing with a couple of well-known country-western groups popular in those days. Eddie Dean had a higher goal in mind apparently. He and his family moved to Los Angeles in 1937 and never left. He worked long and hard and finally achieved his starring roles in several western movies, along with his horse "Topper". He and his family lived very comfortably during his lifelong dream of entertaining. I got to see a few of his movies, and once Eddie came to Dallas to meet his fans at the opening of one of his movies here. In later years I was fortunate enough to accompany my daddy to visit Uncle Eddie in California, where I watched the making of one of my uncle's movies. That was exciting – to actually visit a western movie set and see all the things done to fool moviegoers about some of the action. I wasn't really disappointed – just interested in how they fake some of the action. Uncle Eddie also had a role on the radio show starring a comedian of that day, July Canova. He played her "ranch hand" and sang several times on her program. While visiting my uncle in California, we went to her home and it was magnificent! I had never seen a real star's mansion before, and it truly was beautiful and very large, located on acreage with horses roaming in back.

My Uncle Jimmie passed away at a pretty early age – the only one of his siblings to do so, so young. My daddy also passed away in his 60s. The other brothers and sisters lived into their late 80s or early 90s. Uncle Eddie was in his early 90s when he passed away. One of the things he always called attention to was the fact that he was the 7th son of a 7th son of a 7th son of a 7th son! Imagine that! It must have brought him good luck, because he made a good living doing what he loved. One great honor given to him was from the Academy of Country Music, when he was awarded their Pioneer Award one year. In his later years the Los Angeles City Council paid tribute to him with the Eddie Dean Country Music Star Resolution. He was also honored with his own star on the Palm Springs Walk of Stars. Fortunately, all of his own family was still around to celebrate the occasion, even though Uncle Eddie had passed away at that time. But the really big award that I think is important is that a song he wrote was entered into the Country Music Hall of Fame – "Hillbilly Heaven". Eddie sang "Empty Saddles In the Old Corral" at Western Star Tex Ritter's funeral, also. Another song Eddie wrote, that rocker Jerry Lee Lewis later made famous, was "One Has My Name, The Other Has My Heart". He wrote that song with the help of his wife, whom he always referred to as "Dearest". In fact, everyone called her that. She has also passed away now. They were one couple in the entertainment business whose marriage lasted all those years until they were both very old. They survived the Great Depression with Eddie and his brother Jimmie helping make people happy with their beautiful voices and ability to entertain. It helped take folks' minds off of some very hard times. That is one of the reasons I pay tribute to them in my writing here. Two Texas farm boys who made good, making people happy. Can't get much better than that!

One trip Uncle Eddie made was with the very popular western star, Gene Autry. He was staring at a rodeo in an Oklahoma town just across the border from Texas. My uncle was a featured singer at the rodeo. My daddy drove us to the little Oklahoma town, and I got to brag about meeting and having breakfast with Gene Autry. Kids these days probably know him for his recording, made several years after our breakfast. It was the popular Christmas song, "Rudolph the Red Nosed Reindeer". I just knew him at the time as a "rootin tootin, pistol shootin' cowboy" who was always the good guy who won in western movies.

Several times when both my uncles were traveling around singing at various events, they would come through Dallas and come by our house for short visits. Even though I was in awe of their entertainer status, the thing I remember that made me really happy when they came to visit was what they brought me as a gift. They discovered that I loved Fig Newton cookies, so each time they dropped in for a visit, they brought me boxes of those cookies! I loved my "famous uncles", but when I was a little kid, I really loved those cookies even more. I suppose these days, Fig Newtons are a staple in many homes, but back in the Depression years, they were a real treat that was too expensive to be enjoyed everyday.

If you are interested, there is a website all about Eddie Dean on your computer, search "Eddie Dean Western Movie Star" to read several items about him and to see some of his movies. There still seems to be quite a following of his life's story – country farm boy makes good entertaining, making movies and singing. Unknown to me a few years ago, one of his guitars was auctioned on the internet, and my daughter happened onto the site and followed the bidding progress, and eventually made the winning bid. I have no idea what she paid for it and she wouldn't tell me. I was surprised and overwhelmed when she gave Uncle Eddie's guitar to me as a Christmas present. Almost as happy as I was once with my gift of those cookies. How great is that!

Sharon Street

Our New House On Sharon St., The Neighborhood, and the Posse That Ran It

The summer before I was about to enter second grade, my parents purchased a new home. They had previously bought a pretty brick home before the Great Depression began. Then my daddy's salary was cut in half and to make things worse, my mama found herself without a job. At about that same time, they discovered I was on the way. So they were forced to give up the nice home and rent a smaller frame house. But as the economy improved and my daddy found a better paying job (one that he had always wanted), the opportunity came for them to again purchase a home. This house on Sharon St. was not a brick house, but it was a pretty white frame house and brand new. My father built a white picket fence around the back yard, also, making it picture perfect.

Most of the houses on Sharon St. were older homes, with a few new bungalows, like the one my mama and daddy bought, scattered throughout the neighborhood.

At our house, as you entered the front door off a small front porch, you came directly into the living room. It was a fairly large room that featured a wide floor to ceiling front window. My mama kept this room closed except for special occasions or when we had visitors. Therefore our new furniture always looked new. One piece of furniture was a large, 5-foot tall, 1920s style mahogany cabinet that housed a record player where we played the 78s of the day. I can remember this piece of furniture from my earliest days. It was not a new piece, but it was a beautiful piece. Actually it was the only one of its kind that I have ever seen. I wish I still had it. To operate the player you had to crank a handle on one side to wind it up before turning on the turntable. It was necessary to keep turning the crank occasionally, as we played those old 78s, to keep that old turntable turning. When you lifted the lid and propped it up you saw on it the picture of a dog listening to an "old fashioned" player with the large funnel shaped listening device. Under the picture was printed "His master's voice" I think it was an RCA Victor Victrola. That old player was fun but also a pain in the neck – or arm- to keep cranked up. My daddy was very proficient in electrical jobs to be done, and one day he decided to convert this player to an electrically run piece of equipment. Apparently he knew what he was doing, because it ran perfectly off electricity after his expert renovation. Several years later a school classmate moved into the neighborhood and taught me to dance listening to the records we played on that beautiful old player. I have often wished I still had it.

The kitchen in this house was right off the living room at the front of the house. It was covered with the linoleum flooring of the day. It had the only dining area in the house. There was a large bay window overlooking the front yard, and our dining table was placed in front of it. There was a large combined kitchen and dining area that provided plenty of room for occasional family get-togethers. There was a side door to the kitchen, which opened onto the driveway down a couple of steps. At the back of this kitchen was the area where my mama had plenty of room to cook and for me to play in the middle of the floor occasionally. Along the wall next to the driveway were the storage cabinets. There was no large pantry in this house. Between the wall cabinets was a window looking out over the driveway toward the house next door. Below that window was the sink and "drain board" made of wood – no granite in those days. Below all this was a bank of lower cabinets. More cabinets than in the house on Wilton St., but no match for storing things like that pantry on Wilton. Along the back wall is where our pretty old Detroit Jewel gas stove stood. You have already read what it looked like. Evidently it was a good one, because we brought it with us and it always stayed there in our kitchen cooking up the most delicious things you could imagine. Mama was an excellent cook! On the wall next to the living room door coming into the kitchen, was where the refrigerator sat. We had a new one by that time. No round thingy on top of this one. It even had a very small freezer compartment where we made popsicles and stored ice cream and made ice in little ice trays. Really uptown! Most of the time, I didn't like to take the time to eat – too busy running around being a kid- so my mama would put a bowl of water in the refrigerator to chill and filled it with cut up raw veggies I could come and go and grab a handful of those "nibbles" and take them outside with me to munch on anytime. I loved raw veggies, and probably got a lot more nutrition that way anyway. Smart mama! On the other side of that door coming from the living room was another narrow little door. When you opened it, a small ironing board could swing down from the wall with a leg that folded down to support it on the floor. A pretty innovative idea for that time. Wish they still did that. Beside that was another innovative idea for that era – a wall phone! In those days they were all black – no color choices. Most people had what we called a "party line", which meant that someone else could be talking on that same line when you picked up the phone to use it. Even though we had different phone numbers that rang only in our individual homes, there were other people using the line whenever they chose to do so, as long as the other party was not using it. So, if you picked up the phone and heard someone speaking on it already, you just said, "pardon me" and hung up and waited. There were sometimes several phone users on the same line. We had a "2-party" line, and that was better. But you always hoped that the other party's conversation would not be long if you needed to use the phone. Thankfully we were lucky in that respect.

At the back corner of the kitchen was the door to my parents' bedroom/sitting room. It was a pretty good size, also. In addition to my parents' bedroom furniture it also held my old "upright" piano against one wall. Sitting atop this piano were my "Storybook" dolls, which were the collectibles of that era. I still have two of them in the old trunk in my garage – Little Red Riding Hood and Bo Peep (minus her sheep, however). I took piano lessons at an early age and can still play one of the pieces I learned for a recital. It is called "Climbing" and runs up and down the scales with a few chords thrown in. Imagine that –70 years later, I can still remember it. I loved pecking on that old used piano, and developed a real love of music by taking those lessons. In front of the piano, was a rocking chair, in the middle of the room, sitting on a thick, heavy round rug. The floors in this house were all hardwood and there was a large room size rug in the living room and various small area rugs in other rooms. The back door of the house was at one corner of their bedroom and opened onto a small open porch with several steps going down into the back yard. The closet in this bedroom was actually a pretty good size walk-in style. Not as wide as some today, but fairly large back then for a closet. There were windows at the back and side of the room. The sidewall, where my piano stood, backed up to the attached garage. Yes, actually an attached garage! Another innovative idea in those days. The only problem was that they had not yet thought to put a door going into it from the house. Had to go out the kitchen door and down the driveway to get to it. But it was "attached"!

Down a short narrow hall and next to my parent's bedroom was the only small bathroom. It had the usual necessities, but the tub was a built-in style with no claw feet or shower. No showers available in bungalows back then. Only soaking tubs. Another missing item was a nice vanity sink with marble or granite top. This bathroom had just a sink with a medicine cabinet over it in the wall. There was a small high window at the back of the room over the toilet. Nothing special there either. The choice of color for these items was white – only white. We've come a long way since then! There was a large linen closet in this bathroom. My parents used to hide my Christmas presents way up in the top of it. They thought I couldn't find them, but I always did. Sometimes Christmas was no surprise. Then my mama got wise and began gift-wrapping them as soon as they were bought and continued to store them up in that linen closet. Smart move on her part, but still a good place to "hide" them.

At the other end of this short hall was my bedroom. It was also a nice size room I had the usual dresser, vanity, bed and bedside table that held a radio and lamp. The furniture was new and up-to-date, unlike my parents' furniture. It was "blonde" wood in a modern style. The outside wall had two windows, one on either side of my bed and two on the back wall, one on either side of my vanity. I had plenty of room to play in this bedroom and it was a nice bright room. I loved it. Plenty of cross ventilation in there, also. We still slept with our windows open in the warm weather, because there was no central air/heat in this house either. As I said before about homes of that era, they didn't install those amenities in houses because it hadn't become something that was available yet. We still just had fans and open windows for cooling and electric or gas room heaters for the cold winters. Along the wall next to the bathroom was my closet. Not a walk-in like my parents' and not large, but adequate.

The garage was a one-car size, as were most garages in those days.

My daddy hardly ever put our car in the garage. He had his "workshop" in there, where he puttered around and either built or fixed things. He taught me and a couple of my neighborhood buddies to build little wooden boats that we floated down the curbs and into the corner drains when it rained.

We had a small, short front yard and a very long wide backyard where my mama hung clothes to dry on the clothesline my daddy had erected for her. That backyard held a lot of things that you will read about in another chapter. No actual playing went on back there, just a lot of work.

The house, as well as the neighborhood, was a wonderful place to grow up and have fun. It is hard to separate the things that happened, because it all just flowed from one activity into another. Even though the country was still "depressed", we kids never were, even without a lot of money to be spent on us. We kept busy inventing our own games and ways to amuse ourselves and just let the adults worry about the rest.

As in the old neighborhood on Wilton St., I had mostly little boys to play with in the new neighborhood on Sharon St., so I was already experienced in boy games and activities. My new playmates were two little boys about my age, so I fit right in. No wonder I grew up a "tomboy". I didn't have a chance to be anything else. Our little posse-of-three were constant companions, roaming the neighborhood without any close supervision. In those days, it seemed that nobody was lurking around seeking to harm or kidnap children. Wherever we went to play, nobody ever bothered us. We felt quite safe from predators. In fact, we never thought about it. Apparently our parents were comfortable with our prowling around all over the place, also. We even rode our bikes about a mile away to a park that had a stream running through it. We carried sack lunches sometimes and ate them while sitting on large flat rocks beside the stream. How great is that! Still, nobody bothered us. (I will tell you about another of our adventures in that park in another chapter.)

Since I was a "tomboy" having no girls to play with, we three little amigos sometimes amused ourselves by sitting my older, worn out dolls up on our pretty, white back picket fence and shooting at them with a BB gun owned by one of the boys. Poor dolls! They had such a good home in my nice room. We didn't have computerized "war games" back then…. shoot, we didn't even have computers! We made up our own shooting games. Our back fence did have a few "pings" in it, as you would expect. After all, we were just kids, not sharpshooters. Just for the record, we never shot at animals or birds or humans with that air rifle – just dolls or targets. I guess we weren't all that bad, and we did have a good time just kidding around in our neighborhood on Sharon St.

Second Grade – The New Brick School Building

Somehow, we all managed to survive first grade in that little old white wooden frame building. One thing that helped us get through it was the promise of a new, large brick elementary school building beginning in my second grade year. This new building would house first grade through seventh grade, and I would attend them all.

We were so excited by the prospect of a new school being built over the summer vacation, that we could hardly wait to be spectators for the event. During that period of time, our little family moved from the house on Wilton St. to the brand new house on Sharon St. How nice it was to enjoy two new structures to begin that year. But the move to the new house made it necessary to ride bikes or walk many more blocks to the new school. As usually seems to happen in construction of buildings, the new school was several weeks late in opening. The old frame building had been removed long before, so we just had to wait for school to open that year. Do you really think any kid minded the summer vacation lasting a couple of weeks longer? No! We didn't care – it just gave us more time to ride bikes to the school site and watch it being built. We weren't allowed close to the actual construction site, but it had a deep front yard, so we sat on the curb and watched it gradually go up that summer. Academically, we had to do a bit of catching up, but we did it successfully with the help of some great teachers.

One thing I remember about this school was how long it appeared. After that old frame building, I guess anything would look long! As you faced the building, the front door was right in the middle, and the first grade room was to the left at the end of the building. It had lots of windows and was nice and bright – a far cry from the old building where I attended first grade. My second grade room was at the back of the building across from the first grade room Then the other grades continued down the hallway on either side of the hall, ending with seventh grade at the far right end of the building, with the music room across from it. We actually had a real music room. Music was my favorite thing and we learned some pretty advanced stuff with this new teacher and our new piano. The younger grades were separated from the older grades by the front entrance and office area. Those older grades were to the right of the office area, as you entered the building. Across the hall from the office were the bathrooms and janitorial area. No outdoor plumbing in this building! The several sinks in the girls' bathroom even had a long mirror over them. A real step up from what we had endured in first grade. And the boys could no longer chase us into them when we were out on the playground. We even had drinking fountains in the hallway at either end of the building, and a couple of them outside on the playground. The cafeteria, which we had never experienced in school, was also across from and down the hall from the office area. It always smelled good passing by on the way out the backdoor to the playground. More about that room in another chapter.

For our comfort and pleasure, the building was cooled in summer and warmed in winter. Now how much more "uptown" could you get than that? Seems pretty basic these days, but it was all we wished for back then. Remember, the depression was still recovering and the WWII was looming.

You could go in the front entrance of the school, across the hall, and out the back door into the school's playground, which had been revitalized with new equipment, and was complete with swings, see-saws, kickball field, and all those modern day (for that era) childhood necessities for us to blow off a little steam at recess. There were other doors at either end of the building, also. So, when we had fire drills, the older children went filing out one end of the building and we smaller kids filed out the other end. For some reason, they never seemed to want us to get together. Guess what. We little kids didn't care! It did seem strange, however.

I loved my teachers, and they seemed to love all of us. We had a modest amount of homework – mostly reading – but the teachers back then really seemed to put forth a great deal of effort to actually teach the subjects in the classroom. We were drilled daily on the math tables. I can remember all of us in class repeating over and over again the multiplication tables. Today this doesn't seem to be the method. However, I know my math tables – addition, subtraction and multiplication – tables from memory without having to give them a second thought. I have tried to pass this along to my grandchildren when doing homework with them over the years, since this does not seem to be what is being done in current day schools. That's a shame. Back in my school days, the objective was to give a child a stable background in the "basics" so that a student could more successfully begin to build on that background. I have seen a lot of things come home in the form of homework for my grandchildren that students of my era were taught thoroughly by the teachers in their classrooms. And as I have remarked before, folks of my generation were some of the most well prepared people for living life, excelling in the workplace, and producing life-improving inventions, that have ever been turned out by our schools. We weren't smarter – just better taught and provided with the incentives to keep pushing and bettering ourselves. Sorry if some of you teachers of today get your feelings hurt by that comment. Instead, maybe you can adopt that same approach and dedication that my teachers had back then. Of course you have to have a lot of cooperation from parents, also, to turn out a bunch of well-educated individuals. My parents and the other parents, when I was being educated in the public school system, seemed to actually care more than some of today's parents. Wake up, folks, and get involved! A couple of my early grade teachers even became friends with my family and sometimes came to dinner at our house. This was probably partly due to the fact that my aunt was a first grade teacher, although at another school close to the area. It was also because they were invited. You might want to try that sometime.

Elementary school was a happy time for me. I loved school, I loved to learn new things, and I loved my teachers. I guess that is why I never got into any trouble and never skipped a day of school. Yes, they paddled kids in those days for misbehaving and breaking the rules – mostly boys. Even though we weren't bad kids, we girls did have one little incident in seventh grade. All the girls got together one day and decided we were old enough to wear makeup, and made a pact to all wear it the next day. Makeup in our minds was to wear lipstick and rouge. We were not into eye shadow or the other face makeup products back then. Our mothers wore powder, but we didn't want to fool with that for our first try at makeup in school. So, we showed up the next day complete with lipstick and rouge amply applied, and we all wore earrings. Of course, this endeavor required us to sneak the stuff on in our bathrooms at home and then leave quickly so that our mama's wouldn't see. That tells you right there that we knew it wasn't something appropriate for us to be doing. We all arrived at school, came to our room and sat quietly at our desks, as was the rule. The boys just stared and laughed. Then the teacher came into the room, glanced around the room, took one look at all the girls, instructed the girls to follow her and told the boys to sit quietly until we returned. We figured we were in for a real tongue lashing for showing up looking like floosies, but instead she marched all of us to the bathroom, lined us up in front of the mirror, collected all our earrings and put them in her pocket, and proceeded to unfurl lengths of toilet paper, put soap on it and wash our faces, one at a time All of that without a word! She didn't have to say anything – we got the point. Then she told us to rinse our faces and to come back to class. With that, she left the bathroom. We didn't have much to say to each other, either. We just did as we were told. She did give us back our earrings at the end of the day. We sure were glad, because they belonged to our mothers. Needless to say, we didn't make up our faces the rest of seventh grade! But when we went to a "Jr. High" in eighth grade, in another school building several miles away, we found that we actually had progressed to the point that wearing a little bit of makeup was O.K. But not the extreme use of it that we tried in seventh grade. We never did find out if our seventh grade teacher told our parents. I doubt it. Otherwise, we would have received some sort of punishment. That old gal knew how to rein us in without any further drastic action. Lesson learned! But, hey, we were just kidding around, and she knew it.

Something we girls never did in elementary school was wear jeans or slacks to school. We all wore dresses or skirts and blouses or sweaters. At our homes and when we were out prowling around the neighborhood it seemed to be O.K. to wear jeans, or even shorts in warmer weather. But when we went to school, we girls never wore anything but dresses and skirts. We actually tried to wear jeans one day in seventh grade, but after taking notes home from the teacher, we all reverted to wearing dresses and skirts again that year. It seemed that girls wearing jeans to school with the cuffs rolled up was a distraction in the classroom. Actually, I cannot remember girls wearing jeans or slacks to school at anytime after that, even through high school. We girls only wore them at home or to picnics or to play in the park. Funny how dress codes have changed. When I picked up my Freshman grandson at high school, I saw everything imaginable being worn by the girls! Just about everything was showing or hanging out! It makes me wonder where their parents were when they dressed for school. Maybe we were just old fashioned, or maybe we had more sense of value back in the "olden days". But then, I remember how our grandmothers wore long skirts and never showed their ankles when they were growing up. My generation had to wear dresses and skirts to school, showing our legs all the way up to our knees. These days some of the skirts and shorts girls wear to school show a lot more than I personally want to see! Go figure – makes me wonder what's next? No, don't tell me. I don't really want to know!

Starting Second Grade
In the new brick building

Three clues tell you it is the first day of school:

1. The sour look on my face
2. The flowers for the teacher.
3. The fact that I have on shoes.

The Lunchroom and The "Poor" Table

In our elementary school lunchroom there was a long table at the end of the room, which sat on a raised platform. That is where the teachers sat all in a row overlooking all the students eating and pulling lunchroom pranks. It was assumed they were also having lunch, but I am sure they were just getting indigestion from all the stuff that we did besides eating during lunch. Those teachers did keep law and order there, however.

The main thing that intrigued me about the lunchroom was a small table off to one side of the room, which was referred to as the "poor table". When you had not eaten something in your lunch that you had not already bitten into, you were asked to place it on that table so that some children could actually have a lunch. Since times were so hard, and many people were cutting back on many things including food, some children either did not have lunch or had a meager amount of food at that meal at school. My family was far more fortunate than that, and even though we did not have a lot of luxuries, my mama always packed me a good lunch. She would fill a sandwich for me with some good ham or meatloaf or some other filling ingredient such as homemade pimento cheese. I liked those things, but once in a while I wanted a good old peanut butter and jelly sandwich, and the "poor table" seemed to have an abundance of them. I think the school cafeteria made them and put them on that table since there were many of them there. I believe some of those children who had less than I did watched me when I went to the "poor table" with my packed full ham or meatloaf sandwich to swap it for one of the peanut butter sandwiches, because some one of them were usually right behind me and swooped down on that delicious meat treat sandwich that I had just laid on that table. I guess they got tired of the same old peanut butter everyday. I didn't do that swap too often, and as far as I know my mama never found out about it...unless one of those eagle-eyed teachers told her. She never mentioned it. But then she wouldn't if she thought I was sharing with someone less fortunate at lunch. It was just a good thing all the way around.

The Bully

When I was in the third grade, I encountered my first bully. His name was Billy and he was the biggest, toughest boy in the class. I still am puzzled as to why he picked me to bully. I wasn't the smallest kid in the class, even though I was probably the skinniest. I guess he just found a way to jerk my chain and it amused him and satisfied his need to bully a victim. I have had encounters with bullying of sorts since then, but not in this exact way, and I learned a lifelong lesson from the incident.

During cold weather I always wore a wool toboggan hat pulled down over my ears to prevent earaches. I always wore this hat when we were out on the school playground. Billy the Bully delighted in jerking the wooly hat off of my head and either running away with it or hiding it somewhere. I would cry and go to the teacher and she would get my hat back – usually in a dirty condition.

One day while out on the school playground, I saw Billy heading my way with his mean grin. I took off running toward the back door of the school to get away from him. He caught up with me and as feared, jerked off my hat, filled it with gravel from the schoolyard, swung it around over his head and flung it up on the roof of the school. Well, let me tell you, at that point I had endured about enough of his bully tactics and decided to put a stop to it! I jumped up at him and planted both my feet right in the pit of his stomach! The mean grin immediately left his face and he hit the ground gasping for breath and holding his stomach. We were in an area where we were more or less out of sight of the teachers on the playground. I actually didn't think anyone was watching and was determined to handle this kid's bullying by myself this time.

But someone was watching! When Billy went down like a deflated balloon, I just stood there for a second wondering what to do next. I looked up and suddenly the school janitor came running out the back door of the school. He looked down at Billy rolling around on the ground, patted my shoulder and told me he saw the whole thing and that he had seen Billy pull off my hat and harass me before. He also said he wondered how long it would take me to fight back and put a stop to the bullying. He said he knew a victim had to show the bully they were not afraid anymore. Then he told me to "scat" and go back around the corner and play with the other children. He told me not to discuss what had happened, and that he would handle the situation. He also said he would get my hat from the roof and put it in my schoolroom. By this time Billy had caught his breath and was sitting on the ground glaring at us. Before I turned to obey my rescuer and get back to the playground, I saw him help Billy up off the ground and I heard him tell him to go to the back door and sit on the steps for a few minutes. Then he followed Billy toward the steps. I went back to the playground and just kidding around again.

I didn't know whether or not the janitor took Billy to the office or the school nurse, but I really doubt that he did. What I did know was that Billy the Bully never bothered me again. In fact, he wouldn't even get close to me after that! One thing I learned that day way back in third grade was how o handle a bully by standing up to him and backing him down. The "Karate kick" probably wasn't the best way, but it was the only way at the time to get him to leave me and my hat alone. I have never kicked anyone else in the stomach (or anywhere else) since that day but I sure learned how to stop the bullying that one runs into occasionally – just back 'em down and show 'em you're not afraid anymore! Works for me.

The Nasty Bird

During school months when we lived on Sharon St., my mama and I occasionally made shopping trips to Dallas after I returned home from school in the afternoon. On these planned trips, I was sternly instructed to hurry and not dawdle on my way home from school, so that we could have plenty of time to do our shopping, since it took at least half an hour on the streetcar to get there. On this particular trip, I was home from school in record time, changed into clean clothes, brushed my hair and washed my face and put on my "nice" shoes. Then we were ready to leave ahead of schedule, and began to hotfoot it the few blocks to the streetcar line. As long as there were passengers waiting to board the streetcar, the operator would stop at every corner if necessary to pick them up. However, if there were no passengers standing there at the corner waiting, the car just sped on by, making it necessary to wait for the next car. Sometimes this was a thirty-minute wait. For that reason, my mama always hurried us to the corner where we would be picked up. There didn't seem to be any apparent "schedule", so it was sometimes a "hurry up and wait" game we played with streetcars. But as far as my mama was concerned, we must always hurry!

On this particular day, we were about a block from our pickup corner, scurrying right along. We had seen the car pass going in the other direction and knew it would soon reach the end of the line where it would reverse its overhead electrical connection and come back our way in a few minutes. On our way to be picked up, we crossed an alleyway opening, right under phone and electric lines on poles that ran down the alley, high up on poles. Just as I passed under these high wires, a bird, who apparently could not hold it any longer, landed on a wire above me and dropped a load of nasty "bird doo" , plop, right on top of my neatly brushed hair! What a mess! I was so overwhelmed and disgusted that I turned and headed back home in a dead run! Well, now, what would you have done? Of course my mama was right behind me, muttering something as we galloped toward home.

Of course, after a good shampoo, which also required a complete disrobing, it was then too late to go downtown to shop. The most disappointing thing about that episode was that we were also going to meet my daddy when he finished work for the day, and go to Dunton's to have dinner and then to a nice downtown movie, afterward riding home with him in our car. I hated that bird! He ruined our afternoon and evening. My mama was really angry, also. It is a good thing my mama didn't pack a pistol in her big old purse, because I imagine she would have picked that nasty bird right off of that wire right then. Lucky, nasty bird!

The Maypole

When I was in third grade, it was decided at school that there would be a May Day program to be held outside on the front lawn of the school. A tall pole was erected, and some of us girls in third grade were selected to dance around it to music, as our part of the program. The pole itself was a tall one, which was driven solidly into the ground after being painted silver. Before grounding the pole, several green silky streamers were attached to the top of it. These streamers had small floral bouquets attached at the end hanging a few feet from the ground. Each girl who was to dance around the Maypole held onto the bouquet end of the streamer while rotating and dancing in a circle around the pole. Get the picture?

Of course these little dancers had a costume and those costumes were beautiful! The parents of each girl were responsible for having the costumes made from a pattern provided by the school's May Day committee. My mama's seamstress was chosen to make the costumes. I was so excited! The fitted bodice was made of some green silky material, and the skirt was made of several layers of an orchid material in a sort of scallop pattern, to resemble overlapping flower petals. The costume was topped off with a green-layered cap that fit closely to the head, with a short stem sticking out of the top. The whole thing appeared to be a picked flower turned upside down, but with legs and arms sticking out. We looked so cute in them!

But then it happened. The day before the May Day program I didn't feel well. Then I began to break out all over. I had caught the chicken pox! No vaccine in those days to prevent that disease – we just caught it and stayed home to get over it. In this case the chicken pox was going to ruin my dancing debut. I was so disappointed and cried for a long time when I found out that I couldn't participate in May Day at the school. However, my mama and daddy did as they usually did and found a way for me to at least see what was going on, even if I could not participate. So, the evening of the program I put on my beautiful flower costume anyway and got into our car with my parents and we drove up to the school and parked at the curb across from the Maypole so that I could watch from the car while my classmates danced around the pole. Since my costume would not fit any of the other girls, they were just dancing one girl shy in the dance production. My streamer hung limply down the pole without me. I don't think most people noticed the problem, but not being included in that dance was one of the saddest days of my childhood. I just had to watch it anyway.

Chicken pox didn't last long and I soon returned to school and to my tomboy duty of being one of the neighborhood tree climbers. So much for dressing up in beautiful costumes and looking girly.

I must say here that I did have one other outfit that was one of my favorites and actually looked "girly", also. It was about the time that Snow White and the Seven Dwarfs came to life in the movie. I think it must have been around Easter time, because I had a white dress with a very full skirt that just topped my knees. It had Snow White and all the Seven Dwarfs colorfully printed all over the skirt. It was so cute! My mama also bought me a bracelet to match, with each character in enameled colors dangling from it. The finishing touch to this ensemble was a pair of white patent leather baby doll (strap on top) shoes. I can vividly remember that outfit. It was so in style.

Of all the clothes I had as a child, most of which were made for me by my mama's seamstress, those two outfits stand out in my memory as the most loved. I have a photo of me in the Snow White dress, but unfortunately I have no picture of the Maypole outfit. I guess my daddy didn't want a picture of me with the chicken pox broken out all over me wearing an upside down flower!

Snow White and the Seven Dwarfs never looked better!
Especially with striped sox and sandals
And don't you just love the hairbow?

Our Shopping Strip
The Grocery Stores, Drug Stores, Café and Movie Theater

Yes, we really had them back in those days during the Great Depression. But they were nothing like the malls or even small neighborhood shopping strips of today.

In my early childhood days, families traditionally had only one car. Therefore, when my daddy was driving our car to work, my mama and I, as well as most of the other mothers and kids, walked to the grocery store or other businesses in the shopping strip closest to our house on Sharon St. Before, when we lived on Wilton St., we could count on my grandmother and her neighborhood store for our groceries, but about the time we moved to Sharon St., my grandmother closed her store and she and my aunt moved to my aunt's new house. My grandmother had extended so much credit to the needy folks that patronized her store during the height of the Depression that it was no longer a means of income for her. People either couldn't pay or moved away and debt collection was impossible. In addition to that, she was getting along in age and really needed the rest and assistance of someone and a place to sit and rock and enjoy her crocheting. (I still have her old rocking chair in my bedroom, by the way, as well as many of her crochet pieces. What treasures!)

Back to the shopping strip, now that you understand why we could no longer shop with my grandmother. Shopping with my grandmother was a short half block to walk, but our new house was a much longer trek of about seven or eight blocks to the small shopping strip that had a small specialty grocery, a drug store, later on a large "super market" a café, a "5 cent and 10 cent store" as well as a small movie theater across the street from all those stores. No jewelry stores or dress shops or shoe stores or candy shops, etc. Just a bare necessities strip. Bare necessities was about the way people had to live at that time in our history. Those who had jobs and any extra money to spend could go downtown to Dallas and shop for other items.

In addition to the extra exercise to go to the grocery and drug stores, it was necessary to drag a wire two-wheeler cart behind you. Going there, it was pretty easy and fun for me to drag or push. But on the way home it was filled with purchased items that made it much more difficult with my skinny little arms and legs to pull and almost impossible to push. My mama always took on that task on the way home. It was much slower going home and got pretty hot in summer and really cold in winter. I was glad when I reached the age when I was old enough to remain at home playing with my friends while my mama went to the shopping strip. We kids quite frequently stayed back at home when our mothers went together to shop those few blocks away, and that will be another adventure tale in another chapter. As everyone knows, when kids are left alone to their own devices, they will likely do something stupid. We did, but more about that later.

Mr. and Mrs. Grisaffi owned the small grocery, which was no more than a little hole in the wall. That may not be the proper spelling of their name, however. That store was the first one we came to on the strip. It had dark, wide wood planks for flooring. I cannot recall all of the products we purchased there, but I do remember that we sometimes purchased meat products. I also remember that my mother visited with the husband and wife owners each time we shopped for groceries. My mama loved to visit with folks. She was a people loving person who loved to laugh and chat with folks. Everybody loved her for that. She had an honest love of people and tried to let them know it wherever we went. What a nice legacy.

Next door to the Grisaffi's grocery, walking down the strip was the small corner drugstore and ice cream parlor. It sat at sort of an angle with the door facing the corner. I think most folks went there, as we did, for the ice cream. Later on another drugstore (no ice cream) sprang up across the narrow side street as you walked toward the end of the strip. It functioned primarily as a prescription and drug products store, as I remember. I remember my mama buying bandages there and also cough syrup.

As you continued down the strip, which incidentally was only two short blocks long, you came to a variety store which was better known back then as a "five and dime" store. It was brimming with cheaply priced "stuff" of all kinds, from balloons to thread to candy to fake junk jewelry. Just walking those aisles and browsing was a treat even if nothing was bought. We purchased few items there, with the exception of an occasional penny candy or a balloon. Penny candy? Unheard of these days, but quite common back then. And I will tell you later how we used those balloons. It came under the heading of stupid kid tricks.

A little while later they built a new "super market" at the corner of the far end of the shopping strip. However, even when we shopped there, we always took time to visit with the Grisaffis first. Today's super grocery stores have entire counters from floor to as far up as you can reach loaded with every kind and brand of cereal devised by man – usually on both sides of the aisle. Our neighborhood super-duper grocery back then only had aisles about one-fifth the length of the smallest market's aisles today, with only about eight feet devoted to cereal selections. That included both cold and hot varieties, but no cereal bars or anything resembling them. Some cereal genius came up with that idea later. The most popular brand was Wheaties. It was touted as "The breakfast of champions" and the box had photos of well known sports figures and Olympic stars on the outside. Those were good flakes and we ate a lot of them. However, it was necessary to add your own sugar – no artificial sweetener or honey was used on cereals back then. We just spooned on a lot of pure sugar. It's a wonder we weren't all diabetics! In many of the cereal boxes, both cold and hot varieties, there were small prizes to entice the kids to beg their parents to buy that brand. We also ate the "snap, crackle and pop" brand as well as a couple of the hot cereal brands. My mama showed no favorites. It wasn't hard to do. There just weren't that many selections in those days.

Washing powders also had a limited selection. These boxes also contained prizes, except that these prizes were geared to entice the adults. Those boxes contained pieces of glassware or small dishes and also dishtowels. Money was still tight and this marketing plan using these little extras or "freebies" was the method used to direct buyers toward a particular product. The store was full of all sorts of new items and it was necessary to be carefully selective so that the small family food budget was not exceeded. It was fun to walk around in there just shopping and seeing a lot of new items, even if we didn't splurge on them.

Around the corner from the supermarket was a small café that served chicken fried steak and barbeque and other delicious foods. It was a real treat in those penniless times to be taken out to dinner at a cafe. It was usually a celebration of some kind to go for a steak dinner. My daddy took us out to that café for dinner one evening. I didn't know what the occasion was that we were celebrating at the time, but as we ate our meal, I quickly found out. It was an unpleasant surprise that made me stop eating when I heard it. This news comes up in another chapter. Read on…

Now back again to our shopping strip. Across the street from it was the local movie house. If memory serves me, it was called the Sunset Theater. But all the kids in the neighborhood, as well as my parents, always referred to it as the "Bloody Bucket" because they showed so many cowboy shoot-em-up movies and scary films. It had the usual popcorn and candy counter in the lobby, which was about one-fifth the size of those counters in the downtown theaters and could be put into one corner of today's theater refreshment and food counters. A big bag of popcorn was 5 cents and so was a drink. The price of candy depended on what you selected and would cost from 1 cent to 5 cents. The price of a ticket to the movie was 10 cents. So for 21 cents you could see a movie and all the other things shown, have popcorn and a drink and even candy if you bought one of the penny varieties. This theater featured a main attraction movie, which was always followed by cartoons and "to-be-continued" serial movies, and coming attraction ads. No business advertising in this theater, of course. Often they showed "double features" as well as other entertainment. So a kid could spend most of a day at the movie theater and have enough food to keep satisfied for about 32 cents. This small theater even had a balcony, which I was forbidden to occupy. This was more of a safety precaution decision made by my parents, when I was allowed to go to the theater alone. I suppose they wanted to prevent me from falling over the balcony. We were never approached or bothered by any strangers bent on harming us, unlike occurrences of children being molested when left alone to watch a movie these days. I often wonder where those mentally screwed up people have originated these days. We kids never encountered one of them back then. My only mishap while watching a movie there was having a wad of bubble gum land in my hair after some kid flung it from up in the balcony.

Not an arrest able offense and I never discovered who did it. It sure gave my mama fits trying to extricate it from my hair!

That shopping strip and movie house weren't much, but they were all I needed at the time. As the song says, I loved it and that's all I needed to know.

Braces

I had beautiful "baby teeth". My mama and daddy had sets of perfectly aligned teeth. I didn't even have a cavity until I was grown and veered away from much healthier eating and tooth care, as well as the discovery that I could eat a lot of candy when I wanted to do so. My daddy had such perfect teeth that he didn't have a cavity his entire life! I guess bad dental habits were not on his "A" list. However, when my "permanent teeth" began to show up, it became apparent that braces were in my future. The clinical word for my problem was "overbite". The usually used word for this was "buckteeth", not a bad condition, but noticeable just the same. And my two front teeth were...shall we say "prominent". So, in elementary school I underwent the obnoxious and sometimes even painful, installation of braces.

The orthodontist's office was not close to home, so periodically my mama and I hopped on a streetcar and paid him a visit. These visits were to verify that everything was progressing and that all wires were in their proper places, and to tighten them unmercifully! The only thing I liked about those visits was the reward from the dentist if I didn't complain during a tightening. He had small figures of Snow White and the Seven Dwarfs that I could take home and paint and put in my room as keepsakes. Needless to say, I had all of them, plus some other figures of small animals, etc. We paid a lot of visits to that dentist!

I had a full mouth of braces – upper and lower. To add to the inconveniences of wearing braces in the first place, I had to wear those small, round rubber bands which were stretched from upper to lower sites, in order to speed up the process of producing a perfectly aligned set of teeth, while at the same time reducing the overbite. The little rubber bands didn't produce pain in the mouth, but they sure were a "pain in the you-know-what"! It was necessary to carry a small envelope of them around with me at school to replace them if they broke. And break they did! They broke when I opened my mouth wide to sing in music class. Several times, the classmates on the row in front of me got pinged on the back of the head with a flying rubber band when one of those little bands rocketed in their direction as I opened my mouth to sing!

I am sure that was annoying to them, even though they laughed. However, the worse problem for me was lunchtime, when I removed the little bands so that I could eat. I would put them on a napkin on the open lid of my lunch kit. Those cute little bands attracted the little fingers of my lunch mates like magnets! One thing I was warned not to do was put them back into my mouth after those grubby little germ-laden fingers had picked them up and played with them. Sometimes they even used them to shoot at each other. So, if I was not quick enough to retrieve them before a curious kid passed by and touched them, I had to trash them and go to my little envelope and get two more. I hated those darned things, but they did keep my friends entertained at lunch.

I wore those braces for years, even into my ninth grade in high school. I had regular appointments every two weeks during school days. I had to miss part of lunch and a study hall to hop on a streetcar and go to the orthodontist. This regularly made me late by about 5 minutes getting to my next class, which was History. The teacher was not one of my favorites and apparently I wasn't one of her favorites. She always made a point of commenting and making it a big deal that I was late one day out of two weeks because I went to the dentist. I always gave her my braces-ridden "cheese" grin as I handed her my late pass and took my seat as the class resumed. Teachers, take note: Please do not do this to kids who wear braces and have to go for checkups, making them a few minutes late for class. That's not "kidding around". That's mean! Braces are bad enough – don't make it worse by calling attention to them!

As bad as braces were back them, and as long as I had to wear them, I am proud of my nicely aligned teeth. I still have a slight overbite, but over the years I have received many compliments on my pretty smile. I guess some things are just worth the effort!

The Woods Behind Our House and What Went On Back There

"The woods are lovely, dark and deep; and I have promises to keep….and miles to go before I sleep…. and miles to go before I sleep" (Robert Frost)

This applied to the three of us, also. We spent a lot of time playing in the woods behind our house. We didn't take a lunch out there, however, because it was too close to home and to the sound of our mamas' voices yelling and announcing "lunch". I wasn't too keen on sitting down to a meal – took up too much playtime. So my usual comment to my mama was that the reason I didn't come when called was that I didn't hear her. She was much more clever than I was, and bought herself a shrill police whistle. You couldn't miss it! Our daddies helped us make a clearing spot next to the little shallow cheek that ran through the edge of the woods. Then they took long, about 2 inch around ropes and threw them over the large heavy tree branches and anchored them with loops. They tied large knots at the end of the ropes that hung down, making a big round seat at the bottom of the ropes. We played "Tarzan" with those ropes. He was a popular movie hero of sorts back then, with an ape for a companion. I think we kids mostly resembled the ape swinging on those ropes instead of the buff, muscled up Tarzan! We had some discarded wooden crates that our daddies got for us somewhere and we used them as table and chairs. A wonderful cool outdoor clubhouse under the trees. A greater kid place to chill out was never devised. We saw a lot of squirrels and rabbits at a distance as we invaded their woodsy home, but we never bothered any of them. For some reason, we were kinder to them than we were to the frogs in the park. There were not many frogs out in our neighborhood woods, but we had an abundant supply of crawdads in the shallow, narrow, muddy creek where we waded often to cool our bare feet. We would swish the water a little to shoo them away when we wanted to wade, because we didn't want to step on any of them and end their lives. So, while we didn't have bullfrogs to antagonize in our woods, we did have those crawdads to play a game with. They seemed to be having fun with us, so we thought it was O.K. We would catch a few of them and line them up on the ground and prod them a little to see which one could win the race to get away from us and back into the creek water. Of course, all their racing prowess was accomplished going backward! It took us a couple of attempts at this to figure that out. We didn't hurt the little crawdads. They had nothing to do all day anyway, so maybe we gave them a little diversion or entertainment in their dull aquatic lives, maybe even a bit of exercise. But I'm sure those little creatures were glad when we got away from that creek and left them alone.

Other creatures we saw occasionally were snakes. Not my favorite playmate, but we did play that same game with them that we played with the bullfrogs. We didn't know what kind of snakes they were. Actually they were water moccasins that appeared when the creek had more water in it so that they could swim around a little while. They had very big mouths! When we saw them and they saw us, they opened those mouths wide and tried to scare us away. We should have taken heed of their warning, of course, but we were invincible – or so we thought. We just threw stuff at them like sticks and they slithered off or swam off and left us alone. However, we didn't wade in the creek when they were around.

One day when we were sitting on our box "furniture" in the woods laughing and talking, the subject of snakes came up. We had seen one a couple of days before and were bragging about how we chased it away. The idea sort of made its way into the conversation that we could bring some of that air rifle ammo (BBs) with us next time we came to the woods and try the game with the snakes that we played with the bullfrogs. It was one of those "what are we going to do next to amuse ourselves" ideas which got unanimous approval from the three of us. Although we never did get close to those snakes, we could fling those BBs pretty far, so we thought it would work.

In a few days, after it showered a while, we knew the creek would have more water. One evening, while we sat on the front steps of one of my pals, we began discussing our snake vs. BBs project. This boy's daddy was sitting in their living room with the door open and apparently overheard our plan, but he didn't say anything to us at the time. A couple of days later, on Saturday, we gathered up our ammo and took off for the woods. Unknown to us, our pal's daddy saw us get the BBs and after we left for the woods, he surreptitiously followed us. We were so absorbed in our project that we didn't even know he was back there anywhere. As we arrived at the creek, we immediately saw one of those big snakes sitting on the bank, partially laying in the water. He saw us, too. Then he opened that wide cotton looking mouth at us and began to crawl toward us. That was different! They usually slithered away. Of course we fired a few BBs at that mouth to change his mind about coming toward us. It didn't work. He kept coming with mouth wide open! We threw handfuls of BBs, and he picked up speed. At that point the daddy came running toward us also and sounded the alarm to run. I didn't waste any time and made a mad dash for safety across the field back toward home. Since I was so skinny and long legged, I was ahead of the race. The boy's daddy grabbed him and was right behind me, with the other boy bringing up the rear. That is just what the snake wanted – just get away from him and leave him alone. We did! After that episode, we three were given strict instructions not to go to the woods when the creek was full and to take precautions not to visit the area before scouting around and being extremely wary of our surroundings. Our parents seemed to forget that we had co-existed with those creatures for a long time before the BB problem. We kids decided that the appearance of an adult on that scene was what made the snake angry – not our hail of BBs at him. Kids are a bit stupid at that age, I guess. However, we were never allowed to take BBs to the woods again. After that experience, we had to ask for the boxes of ammo that our parents had taken away from us.

The moral to this story is pretty obvious!

The Field Behind Our House and What Came Out of It

"The Trap"

In the fields and woods behind our house lived may small animals – rabbits, squirrels, possums, snakes, frogs, crawdads, mice, birds, etc. On one of my excursions through the field behind our house and into the woods to play in the creek, I got the bright idea of making and setting a trap just to see what kind of animal I could catch. I ran back to the house and told my daddy my idea. As usual, he was ready to help me get my project off the ground – or maybe I should say on the ground. He made my trap out of a piece of old chicken wire and shaped it like a long dome. Then he attached it to a board for the bottom and hinged it at the back. We propped it open at the front with a stick and baited it with a little bit of cheese, some apple bites and some lettuce, since we thought that would appeal to most any animal's appetite. This food was put in the very back of the trap so that the animal would have to climb into it to get the food, while knocking the stick aside and thus trapping him in the homemade trap. Then we put the trap out into the field a few yards from the woods. Don't laugh! Lo and behold, a couple of days later when I checked on it, there was a possum securely caught in my trap!

My daddy was at work and my mama wanted nothing to do with a hissing mad possum. I was like the little dog chasing the train – I didn't know what to do with it after I caught it. We had not thought out that part of the plan. I guess my daddy didn't think we would actually catch something with that rickety little trap. Oh ye of little faith. Kids can do anything! Don't you know that?

So I trotted off back across the field and down the street to a neighbor's house, leaving Mr. Possum in the cage. The neighbor's son was a hunter, whose story I will tell later. He grabbed a big cloth sack from his garage and ran back down the street with me. With all this running back and forth, we had gathered a group of kids behind us to see what was happening. When they saw that full trap they were all ready to eat their words. They didn't think I could catch anything either. Our neighbor's son put the whole trap with the possum inside into the sack and carried it back to his house. There was a lot of hissing going on still. So he told me and my friends to just go play and that he would try to safely get the possum out of the cage, calm it down and feed and water it. He had had small animals before, so I knew he could do it. I was just proud of myself to have actually caught something in my trap.

This young guy had a larger cage in his garage from a previous animal, and he pushed the possum into it so he could move around and kept it in his garage and finally got the animal to settle down and eat and drink. It took a while, but this guy eventually made a pet out of that possum. After a while longer, he even allowed it to roam inside his garage on a long very light weight piece of chain attached to a rafter, with the other end attached to a collar around the possum's neck. The animal would climb up onto the detached garage rafters (no finished out garages in those days). When we kids came to visit, it never did get friendly with us. We were pretty loud and rowdy, so I can understand why. Besides, he was probably still mad at me for capturing him. Sure can't blame him for that. But I was a kid with nothing to do and was just kidding around. No harm intended.

Our possum's tether was so long and loosely looped around the rafter that he could run back and forth on his rafter and then climb out of the garage's open door and up onto the roof. It sure was fun to look up and watch that cute old possum roam around on that roof. His new master eventually took him back home to the woods behind our house and turned him loose. We kids all went along to watch him scurry away and up into a tree and bid us "goodbye".

I didn't set any more traps and gave the possum trap to our neighbor. It was interesting while it lasted, but one possum was enough fun! (My nana agreed.)

"The Hunter"

The same young man who befriended and tamed the possum was also a hunter. He was a teen, but he knew how to handle a gun and hunt with it. The woods behind us had many more animals than possums and he helped keep them out of our gardens by hunting them and thinning out their populations. He didn't just hunt for the fun of it. Those rabbits and squirrels out there were good eating! He also loved chocolate pie.

When he was on his way out to the woods to hunt, he would drop by our house, using our driveway as his route to the woods, and knock on our kitchen door, which opened onto our driveway. When my mama answered the door he would tell her where he was headed. That was the signal between them. She would drop whatever she was doing and get out the pie-making stuff, which she always had in the cabinet, and begin baking a chocolate pie. We would hear the gun going off occasionally while the pie was baking. After a while the hunter would come back and knock on our kitchen door again. Then he and my mama would exchange cleaned, dressed, cut up and ready to cook rabbit and squirrel for a fresh baked, made from scratch crust and filling, chocolate pie with a big covering of meringue on top.

I knew then we would have a good dinner that night. The rabbit meat tasted good to me – just like chicken – but I didn't care much for the squirrel. That second chocolate pie she always made was for us to enjoy and it really hit the spot!

"The Pet Field Rabbit"

As I previously told you, when we lived on Wilton St. in my very early childhood, I had a beautiful white rabbit as a pet that came to an untimely end. Then when we moved to Sharon St. with all the field and woods and small animals, I had a short episode of playing mama to a little wild field rabbit. That ended up being a success story with a better ending.

My daddy mowed our yards and also behind our back fence with one of those old rotary blade hand-pushed mowers – the only type of lawn mower in those days. Lots harder and slower and it required more physical labor when mowing. He usually mowed the tall grass behind our back fence to about three or four feet away from the fence. This grass grew much faster than our lawns, so it was much taller than the lawn grass when he found the time to get back there and mow. One day the grass had grown so tall back there that it was necessary to first cut it back with a scythe before he ran the mower over it. As he was hacking away at the tall grass, he noticed movement at the corner of the fence at the far end. When he investigated, out popped a mama rabbit and three of her babies, all scurrying away from him across the field towards the woods. But one undersized little brown bunny was left trembling in the grass. My daddy knew the mother rabbit would not return for it and it was too afraid to move, so he scooped it up and brought it into the house. The poor little thing was smaller than the palm of his hand. Just a little runt. My daddy was very upset just thinking he could have run over it with his mower later and killed it. So, in the absence of its mama, we became the little orphan rabbit's parents for a while. We discovered it was a little boy rabbit, so we named it Mister Bun Rabbit. Not too unique, but appropriate.

We made a bed for the little one out of a box filled with rags and grass. We fed him milk with an eyedropper. My daddy seemed to know what to do for him to keep him alive and growing. Maybe a lesson he learned as a boy growing up on a farm. Anyway, Bun Rabbit thrived and grew. When he was bigger, he was allowed to hop around in the house. There were no wall-to-wall carpets back then in small bungalows – just hardwood floors and kitchen and bathroom linoleum. So it was pretty easy to clean up after him. The only difficulty I had in doing that (because it was my job) was when he decided to spend the day back in a corner of my parents' room under their bed. That required some crawling and scooting to reach the cleanup areas and also to retrieve the bunny to return him to his home in the box.

After a few weeks, that sweet, cuddly little runt became a pretty good-sized rabbit. That was when my daddy and mama decided it was time for him to join his own family unit back in the field and woods. It was hard to give him up, but my parents had all the right reasons and arguments about why it was time for him to graduate to the outside. We walked out across the field one-day carrying him in his box and let him out to freedom. The "wild" animal instinct took over and he hopped away, investigating the ground in the woods. It was hard to walk away, but it was time. Just like when it comes time for our children to leave home. It's hard to give them up to their world, but let them go we must.

God speed, little bunny. It was fun! I just hope he wasn't one of the rabbits our hunter friend brought back to us from the woods. Oh, gosh, don't even think about that!

"The Visiting Snake"

One morning as my mama and daddy and I sat in the kitchen eating our breakfast, my daddy suddenly pointed out the front window toward the sidewalk leading up to our porch, leaped up from his seat and rushed out the back door toward the garage yelling "snake- blue racer". My mama and I looked out the window to where he had pointed and saw a large blue-gray snake laying there. I found out later that a blue racer snake wasn't poisonous, but it sure looked ominous lying across our sidewalk. Then we saw my daddy running around the corner of the house with the garden hoe raised, as he was about to attack the snake. The snake retreated quickly toward our front porch, with my daddy in hot pursuit hacking at it. They reached the front porch and I couldn't see them from my kitchen window lookout, so I ran into the living room and jerked open the front door. About that time the snake had coiled and was about to strike at my daddy and his raised garden hoe. As I opened the door, the snake decided to strike in my direction! I quickly reacted and slammed the door – just about the time the snake's head entered it. I took all the thunder out of my daddy's snake stalking by cutting the head off of the snake, right into our living room. I thought my mama was going to faint! Then she started laughing. My daddy came back into the house through the kitchen door and when he saw what had happened, he also began laughing. He got a grocery bag and opened the door and removed the headless snake from the porch and his head from the living room. What a mess! He wasn't laughing when he cleaned it up, but I felt pretty smug about having beheaded a snake right in my own living room. It sure did ruin a good breakfast gathering, however.

That episode could probably come under the heading of "don't try this at home".

That field held a treasure trove of animal adventures, and I loved them all. What a great place to play and grow up, and what wonderful memories that field made.

Just Kidding Around In The Neighborhood

"Cat. Doll Clothes and the Buggy"

As previously disclosed, my old worn out dolls became the targets of our air rifles and BBs. We did this doll shooting before the snake incident happened which robbed us of our ability to use BBs without permission. So what did we do with the doll clothes – mostly baby doll dresses? That story involved a neighborhood cat. Cats could roam around then, too, just like I see them doing today. Can't put a leash on a cat, I guess. Everybody in the neighborhood fed this cat, even though it belonged to a lady who lived at the end of the block. When you have baby dolls, you must also have a buggy to put them in and push them around sometimes. I had a really neat one with large rubber tires on the wheels. Rolled really well. It had a handle to push it, much like a current day grocery cart. The buggy was made of woven wooden slats and painted light blue. A really cute buggy. But I was outgrowing pushing dolls in it and besides that is not what boys did and I had to conform to their activities if I wanted someone to play with. So one day as we three sat on the curb wondering what mischief we could get into next, a neighbor's cat wandered by. We all always petted him when he came around and rubbed on our legs and that is what he did that day. Suddenly…. birth of an idea! Why not dress that cat in those old doll clothes and take him for a ride in the baby buggy. Yeah, why not?! So we caught the cat and sat it on one of the boy's lap to be petted while I went to get my doll clothes and buggy. They waited on the curb. When I got back and we began dressing the cat in doll clothes, he started to wiggle around. We petted him and talked to him and he actually let us put the dress on him loosely. We had been good kids as far as he was concerned, just petting him and feeding him and talking to him, so he let us continue. But when we put him into the buggy and tried to get him settled down, he began to really protest. The buggy was sitting in front of my house on the sidewalk, which was at the top of the street's incline. I lost hold of the buggy handle while we were trying to get the cat to lay down in it, and off down the hill it began to roll! About halfway down the hill, that cat flew out of the buggy yowling and ran to his home and up the tree in the front yard. The buggy crashed at the end of the street when it bumped off of the curb. It took a while to get kitty down from that tree. His owner chased us away and told us never to touch her cat again. Don't worry, we didn't! That cat never came near us again. I never got the doll dress back, either. We weren't really mean – just full of it!

"Dirt Piles, Kites and Horned Toads"

Since home construction was temporarily halted during WWII, our neighborhood on Sharon St. had several vacant lots in the next block. We had a vacant lot on either side of our house, also. Our daddies kept one of them mowed so that we kids could use it to play baseball. The lot on the other side of our house was used for the "Victory Garden". But the whole block of vacant lots up the street was the most fun and provided the most adventures.

A builder had begun to prepare the lots for building houses, but he was interrupted by the war. He got as far as clearing the field there and dumping many piles of topsoil all over it. That is when his progress stopped, and the small, about four feet high, piles of dirt stayed in that field for a long time. Grass and weed eventually grew over them, but the open spaces were kept mowed. We kids kept most of the "hills" free of vegetation, by running and playing on them. We tried riding our bikes up and down over the little hills, but some were too high and we quickly learned, after a few tumbles, which hills we could use for bike racing. This game soon became old, so we moved on to other activities.

However, we didn't totally abandon the higher hills, which were not appropriate for bike riding. We would use them for cover when we played cowboys and Indians or war games. We sometimes played the Cisco Kid and Poncho (his sidekick). One of the kids had a large sombrero and we took turns wearing it and being the sidekick. We all had a cowboy hat, so we could all play Cisco or the Lone Ranger or whatever favorite hero we were acting that day. When I was much younger, I had a pair of chaps and a Hoot Gibson shirt, but had outgrown them. Hoot was a cowboy star in the old western movies back in the 1930s. I also had a Bob Burns Bazooka at that earlier age to go with my ensemble A Bazooka back then was not a weapon; it was a toy slide trombone-type musical instrument. You blew into it while humming and made a sound like a piece of tissue paper blown on over a comb. Bob Burns was a comedian who used his Bazooka in his act and was apparently smart enough to market similar instruments as children's toys. Very simple entertainment back then. Not many frills.

Now that you are up-to-date on old actors and their props, let's get back to the hills. Another thing we did with those higher hills was fly kites from atop them. We built a lot of those kites ourselves out of newspapers and sticks. Once in a while, we had a store bought kite and when it tore, we saved the sticks from it to construct a new kite, using those newspapers. We didn't waste a thing! My daddy even helped me make a "box kite" using some of those old sticks. We stood up on those hills and sent out kites up as far as the strings could take them. Since there were no houses on the block yet, there were no low electrical or phone wires in the area to tangle up our kites, and we each stood far apart on our own hill so that we never tangled our kites with each other. We collected all the strings we could find and securely tied them together and continued to lengthen them to make our kites soar higher and higher. We would attach small scraps of paper, on which we had written notes, to the string and watch them climb up toward the kites. They eventually blew off, however. Kites were really a lot of fun in the early spring when the weather was windy. It was a shame kite season didn't last longer.

There was a lesson in all this kite building and string saving that we learned, especially during wartime. Even we kids learned to be conservative with our materials.

Something else that we discovered on that vacant lot was an army of little creatures called horned frogs – or Horney toads, as we named them. We had not seen them before the dirt piles appeared, so they must have arrived with the dirt. I have heard on some of the TV programs today that those little guys are becoming extinct. There are even some exhibits housing them in some zoos now. But back then we had an abundance of them living in our piles of dirt. Once they got used to us playing there, and decided we were not there to harm them, they let us catch them and hold them and stroke their soft little bellies. They looked like little dragons with the short spikes on their backs and a larger horn on their heads. You couldn't pet them comfortably on their backs because of those spikes, but they loved their tummies rubbed as we held them in the palms of our hands. What cute little fellows. We liked them and mostly left them alone and tried not to step on them when we played on the dirt piles where they lived. People about my age are about to all be "extinct" soon, also. Maybe we will all be missed. I hope so!

"More Frogs"

Another thing we three kids found entertaining that involved frogs was actually in that park a mile from home. We did ride our bikes there and we did carry lunches with us that we ate on the large flat rocks beside the stream, but we also carried a small box of BBs.

There were also large flat rocks out in the middle of the stream. The trees that lined either side of the creek allowed sparse sunlit spots and when the sunlight reached those stream rocks, several large bullfrogs came out and stretched out on the rocks to sun themselves. Peaceful scene? Not to a band of three with a box of BBs. It was a perfect opportunity to play with the frogs. On a previous visit to the park for lunch, we had thought of a bright idea that involved these big old frogs. Being the scamps that we were, after we knew the frogs were settled there on their rocks, we took out the BBs and tossed them in the direction of the frogs. We were not intending to hit the creatures, just have fun with them. We had, on another occasion, flipped a crumb of bread their way and watched the action. Thus the idea of flipping the BBs to them. They unfurled their long tongues and flopped them out to catch what they thought was a flying insect. They grabbed so many BBs that they were unable to hop. Bad kids! But what did we know. We were just kids out to have fun and eat a picnic lunch in the park. We never did discover what ultimately happened to those frogs, but I can imagine. BBs thrown at snakes, yes – frogs, no. Probably hurling those little pellets at either one of them was not a good idea. We considered the snakes mean and ultimately dangerous. However, feeding the frogs BBs is not an activity I am not proud of now, so I feel the need to confess here. Poor frogs!

"Poison – The Amateur Chemists"

Having two little boys to play with, I had to join in the male-related projects, even the scientific ones. However, I must admit that in this particular instance, I was not only a willing participant; I was also a chief instigator. The project was the creation of "poison". My mama and one of the other mamas allowed us to use their kitchens to mix various liquids and spices and bottle them in old soft drink bottles. This usually occurred on either a rainy day or one that was too cold to play outside. We never actually thought it was too cold or wet to play outside, but our mamas did, and they made the rules. We really loved to play outside splashing around in the rain and getting dirty in the flowing curbs, but our mamas frowned on that happy playtime activity, also, especially when the weather was chilly. So, in bad weather, when we kids tired of laying around on the floor reading and trading comic books, we converged on the kitchen and began to create our latest concoction that we called "poison." We were repeatedly warned by our mamas not to ingest any of the stuff we were mixing. We did, however, sample the mixture we made up with vinegar and baking soda. It fizzed and foamed, and we just had to have a taste. We called it "beer", even though none of us had ever tasted beer. None of our parents drank alcohol, so we were completely in the dark as to what beer really tasted like. We had heard it foamed, so we labeled our mixture "beer" and took a little sip. Wow, pretty potent and nasty stuff! We decided we didn't like beer.

After mixing our "poison", we poured it into whatever empty bottle was available, and corked them. Some had lids and that was really better. If no lids or corks were available for the small mouth bottles, we just got some of the clay we often played with and fashioned a cork for them and let it harden in the full bottle's mouth. After this was all accomplished, we set them aside (usually on the back porch) and waited until the weather was better. Then, after we could play outside again, we took the bottles to one of the boy's back yard. They had a crabapple tree back there which had a lot of dirt and sandy soil under it for some reason – no grass growing there. We took our little shovels and buried the bottles of "poison" in the soil under that tree, like pirates burying their treasure. I have no idea why we picked that tree. Probably because the soil was easy to dig and my mama wouldn't let us bury the bottles under her trees. Or perhaps it was just our "plan" to buy them there in that particular spot. It was also our plan to leave them there for years and then dig them up to see what had happened to our "poison". But we grew up in the meantime and apparently forgot to go back and check on our scientific project. Thinking back, I have wondered if anyone ever dug up that stuff and I would like to know if they were curious about what they thought it was and who buried it there and why. For their information, it was just a bunch of kids doing their thing on a bad weather day.

"The Curbside Fortress"

At the corners of the street, there were drains in the curbs. These were wide enough and long enough in the openings to allow skinny kids to slither down into them. There was enough height in them for us to stand up and peer out of the opening. These drain were directly across the street from each other. We three little soldiers used to take our toy guns with us and choose up sides to fight a "war" in those "bunkers". Of course, one side had to have only one person in the bunker, which was usually me. Guys somehow have a tendency to stick together. We shot at each other, firing and ducking and making gun noises with our mouths. No air rifles allowed in that game! We were so aware of the fighting going on in WWII that we played war games often in those curbside bunkers. However, those drains had another use for us, other than carrying off the water in the curbs and providing a place to hold our war.

During dry weather, my daddy allowed us to use his garage workshop area and he taught us to construct little boats, using scrap wood. We stored them on a shelf in our garage and when a rain shower produced enough water to fill the curbs, we ran and got our little boats and floated them down the curbs on either side of the street, following them, splashing in the curbs behind them. This only happened in warm weather, of course. No wintertime cold weather wading or boating was the rule. Needless to say, when out little boats reached the corner, down the drain openings they went. Then we waited until the weather cleared and the drains dried out, and we slithered into the openings and retrieved our boats. Or rather the ones that were still there. We lost a few boats that way and returned to our garage to build more. No store-bought toys – just homemade little boats to provide fun in the rain. Homemade cost less and was just as much fun in difficult times. We learned to accomplish things for ourselves and be satisfied with what we had. Not a bad lesson, actually.

"More Kid Fun"

There were other more mild activities that we did to amuse ourselves while just kidding around. Some of them were:

Red Rover- Red Rover, Red Light –Green Light, Eeny-meeny-miney-mo, Ring-around-the rosey, London Bridge, Jump Rope, Hot Potato, Hop Scotch, Giant Step- May I, Double Dog Dares, Hide and Seek, You're It. If you don't recognize any of these, ask your grandparents to show you how to play them.

We enjoyed doing several other simple things for entertainment. We didn't have pools, so drinking from the garden hose on a hot day and then squirting each other was what we did to cool off. We also loved to run through the lawn sprinklers in our clothes. We soon dried while running around in the sun. Watching the clouds change shapes while lying on our backs and seeing them form shapes of animals, people, houses, etc. was a way to relax after some hard running and jumping.. We played outside so late the street lights came on. Then, after dark, catching fireflies – or lightening bugs, as we called them – in jars was a favorite pastime. We clipped cards on our bike spokes to make noise. Just sitting in the shade on our porch, licking our fingers after sticking them in Kool-Aid packets to eat the grainy sweet stuff was a real treat.

If you haven't had the pleasure of doing any of these things, then you haven't really enjoyed the simple life of the depression era. It may sound pretty dull to some folks, but it was what we did and we had fun doing it. I wouldn't change a day of it for myself, either. Looking back, even the memory of doing those things amuse me and makes me happy.

Boat Builders

Church Twice On Sundays

In my childhood, our family attended church every week, twice on Sundays and often during other weekly services. My daddy was a Deacon in our church, which was located on Tenth St. in the Oak Cliff area of Dallas. I was told that Tenth St. had more churches located along it than any other street in the U.S. I can't verify that, but I tend to believe it, because there seemed to be a church on every corner along Tenth St. when I was a kid.

All week long in good weather, I mostly ran barefoot inside and outside, wearing what we called a "sun suit" – a one piece shorts/top set. Or maybe I wore a pair of shorts and a sort of midriff top. No designer fashion playwear for kids during the depression. Nobody could afford them – at least not middle class families like mine. However, on Sundays I put on my best dress, patent leather shoes, and clean sox, together with freshly shampooed hair and scrubbed body, and went with my family to Sunday School and "Big Church". We even drove there in our car – not on the streetcar. Sunday was a special day meant for worship, rest and being with family. It was mandatory that I be quiet and reverent in "Big Church", which wasn't easy for a rambunctious kid like I was! But I did the best I could. I really loved singing the hymns and still remember the old ones we used to sing. Churches these days don't dwell on them anymore and I think that is sad. But I guess the message is the same.

After church there was always a big lunch spread, sometimes featuring a roast beef, real mashed potatoes and brown gravy, and fresh cooked veggies, and sometimes even homemade biscuits or rolls. Yum! During wartime, there were lots of things rationed and there was even a day set aside known as "Meatless Tuesday". But on Sundays we usually had a large lunch with all the trimmings. My poor mama, not too much of a day of rest for her, I think. She usually left the roast cooking slowly in the oven while we attended church, so at least that was ready to eat when we returned home.

After lunch, while my mama cleaned up the kitchen, it was time for "lap talk" with my daddy. Afterward, I played around inside the house with things like my wood burning set or coloring books and kept things to a quiet level for the folks. It was also necessary to stay put in the house and stay clean, because there would be another trip to church in a few hours for the early evening service. This service was not as long as the morning service. We went to our age appropriate Bible study for a short time and then to "Big Church" to hear a short sermon. There was a lot of hymn singing in the evening and baptisms of those who had accepted Jesus as their Savior in the morning service. I joined that group of baptized believers when I was about eleven years old. It has been the one outstanding decision of my life and the feeling of closeness to God and his eternal blessings and care have followed me to this very day.

Taking me to church twice on Sunday and the instructing from the Bible at home, and making sure that I understood what being a Christian was all about, were probably the best gift my parents could have given me. Nothing since that time has ever managed to shake that faith my parents helped to instill in me.

Thanks, mama and daddy for that great gift! I have tried to pass it along to my children and grandchildren. It is successfully working in their lives, also.

My Daddy In The Kimono

I loved to comb my mama's and my daddy's black wavy hair. My mama's French ancestry and my daddy's German-Dutch ancestry must have produced the hair color, but I am not clear on where the waves came from in their hair. I inherited my mama's olive skin and my daddy's blue eyes and both their dark hair, but sadly, minus the waves. The term "straight as a stick" certainly applied to my hair. One Saturday afternoon, as my daddy was relaxing in his chair, I was combing and "styling" his hair and pinning it up in all sort of "dos" I had used an old Japanese style kimono from a play I was in once, as a cover for him, sort of like I had seen the barbers use to prevent hair from falling onto men's clothing. Suddenly I got the idea to put his hair up in a spectacular do with an "Asian flair". My daddy was, at this point, dozing because of all the relaxing hair brushing. So, after the hair styling was finished, I decided I would get into my mama's makeup drawer and, while he was unaware of what I was doing, put a little lipstick and powder and rouge on my daddy as a joke. My mama was in the kitchen doing something at the stove, so she was not aware of my project. My daddy was so easy going that I knew he would not get mad and would go along with my fooling around. That is, as long as I helped him wash it all off later. At least that is what I told myself.

About the time all this beauty shop stuff was going on, one of my neighbor pals came over to visit. He about freaked out when he saw my daddy sitting there asleep with all that stuff on him. My mama came into the room and couldn't stop laughing at the whole situation. Then my pal came up with one of his crazy plans. All this laughing woke my daddy up and when he looked in the mirror, he also roared with laughter at what he saw. (I knew he wouldn't really get mad at me.) The Kimono, which came down to my feet when I wore it, was much too short on him and barely came down to the calf of his legs. He was fully dressed, so there were his pant legs hanging down below it. The kimono wrapped all the way around me when I wore it and it tied in the back. But since my daddy was so much larger, it just lapped a bit in front and tied there in a bow over his stomach. My neighbor pal kneeled down and rolled up my daddy's pants legs to under the kimono. So, there he stood, the good-natured sport that he was, dressed like a heavily made up, muscled and hairy legged Geisha girl. He couldn't quit laughing at himself and neither could we.

But that was not the end of my pal's plan for him. My pal told my daddy he thought he should go across the street to my pal's house and knock on the door. When my pal's mother came to the door, he was to pretend to be a fortuneteller and tell her he had come there to tell her fortune. Since my pal's mama was also a good sport, we thought she would get a laugh out of it, too. My mama wasn't so sure, however. It took some talking, but we finally convinced her it would be O.K. The only thing missing was some kind of headgear. So, we took a sheer purple scarf from my mama's collection and draped it over my daddy's head like a veil. Then we went to the garage and got my empty fish bowl and put that upside down in my daddy's hands like a crystal ball, and sent him across the street to possibly either scare the beegeebers out of my pal's unsuspecting mama, or cause her to die laughing at the sight of my daddy.

At first, she started to slam the door when my daddy began his high-pitched fortune teller spiel, and then she recognized who it was and ran and grabbed her camera. He couldn't get away fast enough, and I still have that photo of my daddy being a good sport in all that getup and just kidding around with us kids. What great fun that was!

Now, I ask you: How many daddies these days would allow kids to do what we did to my daddy? And he continued to retain a sense of humor and, immediately afterward, managed to restore his dignity in the neighborhood. Our daddies went way beyond the limit for kids when I was growing up. Taking kids to participate in sports events is one thing, and probably a good thing. But, if you are a daddy, why don't you try kidding around with your children like our daddies did with us. You won't regret it. It will make wonderful memories for both you and your kids.

The War – WW II

As I related in a previous chapter, my daddy took us out to dinner one night at the local café and I didn't know what we were celebrating. As it turned out, it was not a celebration! Here is what happened:

World War II had begun with the Allies (including the U.S.) and the Axis (Germany and Italy) powers at war with each other for world domination. At least the German Nazi Adolph Hitler wanted to rule Europe and England, if not the entire world! His was an evil regime and we were very afraid of his agenda.

My daddy had been a radio operator on a ship in the Navy during World War I, which was supposed to be the war to end all wars, they said. Not so! My daddy was just old enough to be in the military service. In fact, he actually joined the Navy. At that age, my daddy was very skinny and when he could not pass the weight requirement for the Navy, one of the recruitment guys told him to go home, eat a dozen bananas and drink a lot of water, and stay out of the bathroom, and come right back to weigh in again. He did as he was told and when he came back and weighed in again, he barely made the cut. After his training, he was assigned to a ship for active duty. He had always fooled around with radios, so he was a natural to serve as a radio operator on the ship. His ship was just underway and leaving the Harbor in New York when they were sent word to turn around and go back into port because the war had ended in the defeat of the Axis powers. So he never had to go abroad or into combat.

Many years later, during the first part of World War II, the Navy was apparently in dire need of accomplished radio operators, and they had contacted my daddy to ask if he would again serve in the Navy as a radio operator on a ship. That ship would be going overseas, of course. Because of his age as a man with a family at the time and previous years of completed service, it would be a strictly voluntary move on his part, they told him. They sweetened the offer with the promise of an officer's position.

My daddy dropped that bomb on us at dinner that night and after his news, I was unable to finish my meal. He and my mama discussed the situation and then turned to me. I told him I voted "No"! My mama agreed with that decision, and I think my daddy was at that point truly torn between his feeling of wanting to serve his country and his responsibility to his family. After all, he had already served a full term of service in one war when he was not much older than some of the men who were being called to serve in the military in WWII. They called it the "draft" at the time. Something no longer in practice in this country. His would be a strictly voluntary decision. He didn't really have to go. It was a tough decision for him, but because of my mama's and my urging, he turned it down. I am patriotic, but I have to say I am still glad he turned it down, especially because of what happened in later years…in a later chapter.

My daddy did, however, serve his country during WWII. He served in our neighborhood for several years as an "Air Raid Warden". That meant he and one of the other dads living near our house were responsible for serving that neighborhood in the event of an air attack by the enemy. What a scary thought for a child my age! When practice raids were performed, he and the other dad went throughout our neighborhood making certain either all lights were turned off in homes or that blackout shades were pulled to block out any light. They ran through the blocks in our neighborhood with small shielded flashlights pointed at the ground checking on the situation. Our government and military leaders were concerned that an air attack might occur, and all homes and businesses were to be shut down to total darkness at night during these practices, so as not to offer any stray enemy planes a target. The Wardens also had buckets of sand that were at hand. I never did understand the reason for them. Probably to throw on a fire. I still don't know. They were also schooled somewhat in search and rescue procedures, just in case an attack did occur and buried someone in the debris. I ran behind my daddy out there in the dark, both of us dressed in dark clothing and hats, checking out the houses to make sure they were darkened. Even the streetlights and any fireplaces were shut down. Gosh, that was a scary time, especially for kids who had spent the day kidding around. Then part of the night was spent hovering in darkness, until the "all clear" signal was given. That's why I always wanted to follow my daddy on his rounds. It gave me something to do besides hover and worry in a dark house!

We never were attacked, but you can rest assured we were ready – or at least we believed we were. I heard in later years that if Hitler had paid attention sooner to the German rocket scientist Von Braun, the U.S. might have been hit with rockets, much like the Germans bombarded the English in their country. What a great day when Von Braun came on over to our side!

Later we were all so happy and relieved one day when we heard shouting outside and looked out to see a newsboy trotting down he street carrying his bag of newspapers and waving one and shouting that the war was over in Europe! Remember, we had no TV back then and not everyone had a radio and those who did didn't leave them on all day. What an amazing day that was! We all just danced around in our yards whooping and hollering.

But unfortunately we still had one more enemy to defeat – Japan. Which leads to another memory of the WWII era.

One of the most vivid memories of WWII was the testing of the atom bomb in various locations. We listened with rapt attention to our radios when this occurred. It was unimaginable that such a bomb was even possible. Without TV back then, we had newsreels about the war shown in our larger movie theaters in Dallas. There was even one theater that exclusively showed newsreels. We all flocked there to see the atom bomb exploded for the first time. It was overwhelming to see those mushroom clouds rising from the bomb site. It sure beat the radio sounds of an explosion by a long shot! But we all still had no idea what that means of destruction was all about. We had a clue when they blew the Bikini Atoll out of the water, however. We knew this was quite a monumental achievement, but the magnitude of the ultimate bomb had still not dawned on us.

When the Japanese came out of nowhere and attacked Pearl Harbor in Hawaii on December 7, 1941, our hearts sank. It was so terrible to imagine what we were being told, but then to see in newsreel pictures what actually happened was horrifying! This attack seemed to hit us much harder than the war in Europe, even though we had seen in the newsreels how bad that was for our military and how badly it had hurt our families and how long it had lasted. This was a sneak attack and not expected. We just were not ready mentally for that. Even though it was many miles from the United

States mainland, it was part of our own country that was being attacked. I remember President Roosevelt saying in his speech telling us about the attack that the day would live in infamy. Now it has all but been forgotten after the September 11, 2001 attack on the World Trade Center in New York – right on our own soil. But as a child back then it was a very scary and uncertain time. I think it brought us all even closer together than before. I have photos on my computer now of the horrible destruction of that attack and I look at it occasionally just to remember how strong our country was, to be able to survive all of that evil adversity back then as we were slowly recovering from the Great Depression.

"Rationing"

Several items that are very common and deemed necessary for living our daily lives today were actually rationed during The War. There were little books in which were stamps to be used periodically for these rationed items. I didn't have to worry about keeping up with that aspect of our lives back then, but my mama and daddy, along with everyone else, were forced to comply with the rationing program. Some of the items that were on the rationed list were sugar, gasoline, tires, silk hose, and several other items necessary to help provide war related necessities. The gasoline and rubber for tires is pretty obvious as some things necessary to be used in fighting a war. But how about silk hose? In those days there were no nylon hose for women. They all wore silk hose. Parachutes also were made of silk then, so ladies either had to go bare legged or use some of their stamps for hose, which they protected as if they were their own children! And that was when a few pair of silk hose were even available. When they were in stores, the lines sometimes wound around the corner to get into the store to buy them. When they ran out of silk hose, it was back to bare legs again. What a long way we have come from silk hose and garter belts to hold them up (which also contained rubber), to panty hose made of nylon, to currently back to bare tanned legs for most ladies. Well, they say "what goes around comes around", so it is not too surprising, and today women don't have to have that extra thing around their waists holding up the hose! My, my, what progress we have made!

"War Bonds"

It is expensive to fight a war. However, it did help boost the economy in this country as we were recovering from the Great Depression. The war effort provided additional jobs for those too old to be drafted into the military service, or those with some disability that prevented them from going to war, as well as jobs for many women who, for the first time in their lives, went to work in defense production factories helping make the machines and guns and other items necessary to fight a war and win. It was also necessary to issue bonds, known as "War Bonds", to help finance the war. When I was in elementary school, I remember buying stamps to paste into a small book. These stamps eventually added up to a War Bond worth $18.75. Later, at maturity, the bond was worth $25.00. We had a weekly banking session in school, when we put into our savings accounts a dime or thirty cents or whatever we had. This was done to teach us the value of saving and was overseen by the school system. We each had a personal account into which our small change was deposited and we earned a small interest rate on it from one of the local banks. This practice continued on into the upper grades of school. The school yearbooks even had a notation after our names that we were a "100% Banker" if we continued to participate. When we were old enough to make the decision, we could withdraw our money ourselves if we wanted to do so. I don't know why that was discontinued, because it seems to be a good way to teach children to save. This event happened first thing in the morning one day each week. During WWII, this banking session was also the time when we could buy another stamp to put into our little books toward saving for a War Bond. When the book was full, it was forwarded to the agency handling this savings project, and in a few days you would receive your bond to be held for several years until it matured and reached the $25.00 goal. This War Bond stamp-buying activity also succeeded in allowing even children to participate in the war effort and helped all of us to stay positive about helping our country succeed. I wonder why this practice was also stopped after the war was over. It would still be a good teaching tool for kids to take advantage of in classrooms. I guess, unlike most of the other economic stuff being spread around today, it is too simple. Back then, simple got the job done! The good guys won!

"The Pile"

Because of the great need for metal during the war to manufacture the necessary war machines, our elementary school had a "metal drive". We all brought all manner of scrap metal objects to throw them on a large pile on the front lawn of the school.

This even included empty toothpaste tubes. In those days they were not made of plastic. Our toothpaste came in sort of a heavy tinfoil tube that you could roll up from the bottom as you used the toothpaste. When the paste was used up, you were left with a small rolled up piece with a cap on top. The tinfoil was added to the pile in the schoolyard. Those pieces of metal objects such as pieces of pipe, old bed springs, iron rods, etc. were picked up by men in a big truck every so often and hauled away to be sorted and melted down to be re-used to make tanks, planes and other war machines. Everyone in the area participated in this effort. The pile grew as high as a house roofline at times. We kids even searched various vacant lots and fields for anything we could find to carry or drag to put onto that metal collection pile. That was a time when every man, woman and even children came together to do what they could for the war effort. Never in my lifetime have I seen such unity of purpose. We joined together in the total war effort like our very lives depended on it. I guess they did! And it worked…. we won. Wake up folks – see what people of like mind that have courage and purpose can accomplish when they unite!

"The Garden"

Behind our elementary school playground was a vacant patch of land. During the war we used this land for a school and family effort to grow what was called a "Victory Garden". The land was tilled and we kids helped weed it and made the rows ready for planting vegetables. We watched things grow and helped weed and water the garden. Later we helped pick and harvest what we had grown. I know it took a lot of food to feed our military people fighting the war, but I never found out exactly what eventually happened to those veggies we grew and picked. Some of them may have been used in our school cafeteria. Some may have been given to families in need of food. I just don't know. I think that keeping everyone, even the kids, busy uniting and bonding for the war effort were one of the objectives of growing our own gardens. Some things were scarce in the groceries during the war and many folks, our family included, had their own gardens at home. Whatever the reason for the school garden or the ultimate destination of the veggies, I loved it and it did indeed bring folks together and keep us united, busy and believing we were doing something useful to help our country at war.

"Our Own Victory Garden":

There was a vacant lot next to our house on Sharon St., since there was no home building going on in the area during the war. Many of the supplies going into home building were being used in the war effort and most of the younger men who worked in the home building industry were off fighting that war. The lot was just sitting there needing to be mowed once in a while. My daddy usually took care of that for the owner when he mowed our own lawn. After the school victory garden sprang up, my mama had the bright idea of calling the owner of this lot to ask if we could till it up and plant a garden there for the time being. He was agreeable and let her use the space for no charge. And why not? It would keep the soil alive and not just sitting there growing weeds.

Some of our neighbors also wanted in on the garden, and it was a nice large area, so why not all join together and plant all kinds of veggies. Even we kids got into the act. The men tilled it up and cleaned it off with our limited assistance. After all, that was a lot of work and we kids hade a lot of playing to do! But we all did our part off and on. After the plot was prepared for planting, I remember dragging a hoe down the length of the lot making rows. My mama and daddy knew I couldn't make a straight line, and since my daddy was somewhat of a perfectionist, he measured the space between the rows and they strung strings at intervals spaced out along the length of the lot and I carved out those rows right beside them. After that, we all bought our seeds and plant starters and all had a very nice garden spot. We also put up stakes for each family's area with their names on them. Some liked lettuce and others didn't, so all had their own spots. Ours, of course, was right next to our driveway close to our house, because we thought of it first. We all tended to our own areas and used our own hoses to water, some dragging theirs across the street to keep their plot moist. My mama grew everything you could imagine in her three long rows and the whole thing was really beautiful. One prob lem we had to solve, however, was the appetite of the rabbits and birds that came in from the field and woods behind us. We staked out several spots and tied flapping strips of some white cloth on them. That didn't really stop the invasion. But we were shooing them away during the daytime when we could. The rabbit raids usually came during the night, especially on the lettuce, and there was not much we could do about that. We humans also got a lot of fresh, delicious veggies from that garden!

My mama couldn't seem to stop planting that year. My daddy also tilled up about a third of our backyard for a spot where my mama could have her corn, tomatoes and okra plants. I loved eating that sweet corn and also the okra. I didn't mind picking the corn, but I hated trying to pick that okra! It really would sting your bare arms. I had to wear an old long sleeved shirt to do that okra picking. But it sure was good eating! And there is nothing better than tart slices of salted homegrown tomato to top off a meal. Now I will have to admit that those really were the "good old days" with regard to our homegrown and home cooked meals. There was only one problem that occurred with vegetable preparation. It happened when my mama was canning some of our homegrown tomatoes. This required the use of a pressure cooker, which held the canning jars and was heated atop the cook stove. This sealed the jars. The cook had to have sort of a precise management of this process, however. If she didn't have the lid of the pressure cooker on properly, or if she took it off before the cooling was finished, disaster happened. One time while canning tomatoes, my mama made one of these mistakes. The lid blew off! Have you ever seen tomatoes spread over a kitchen ceiling? I have! She and my daddy finally got it all washed down and repainted. We didn't mention it after that. We just had fewer tomatoes to eat later.

Behind our backyard garden, my mama planted a peach tree and a cherry tree. Of course the birds always beat us to the fruit. I think I may have had the good fortune to pick a couple of cherries and a few peaches before they got to them. If it wasn't the birds in the peaches, it was the worms. We were definitely not good fruit tree farmers! Another tree growing just behind our back fence with its branches hanging over it into the yard was a Bois d'arc tree - you know, "horse apples". You couldn't eat horse apples, but they were fun to pick and throw out into the field behind us. My job was to keep the ones that fell into the yard thrown out into the field. The tree provided a little spot of shade for us kids to rest in occasionally, so nobody cut it down. Besides, the branches were convenient to hang onto if we decided to climb over our little white picket fence to run over the field behind our house to play in the woods.

More About WWII Planes in the Field

One exciting feature of WWII that we kids witnessed first hand was the training of pilots in those little yellow open bi-planes. Bi-planes, for those too young to know, have two wings, one of them above the cockpit, the other divided on either side of the plane These wings were attached to each other with vertical supports between them. The plane also featured an open cockpit with the pilot in full view. My favorite plane during the war was the P-38, which had two "tails" with a fin on each tail. They looked so sharp! We kids all had kits to put together some of these planes, also. It was all about the war in those days. I guess it had to be, but kids had a way of inserting play into it.

The wide-open field directly behind our house on Sharon St. was where only Johnson grass and other weed grew. This field, where we kids frequently played had no real use at the time. This grassy space was about 30 yards wide. I never measured it, but my memory of how long it took us to run across it to play in the woods tells me it had to be at least that wide for what was about to occur.

For some reason the military decided that particular wide, flat field which was three suburban neighborhood blocks long was the perfect place for pilots to train and learn to dive down, land, roll and then immediately take off again. Someone told us they were Navy pilots. Maybe they were practicing taking off and landing on carriers. I still don't know that answer. Of course the military people didn't confide their plans to us.

These planes were powered by engines using propellers. No jets then. They made the kind of noise that propeller driven planes make. It was pretty noisy in an otherwise quiet neighborhood and brought the war closer to home to us more than anything else. We kids were warned to stay away from the practice field during their training periods. Of course we never disobeyed and ventured out that way, especially when we heard the sounds of the engines roaring coming toward the field behind our homes. We weren't stupid – nobody wanted to get run down by an airplane! It kind of hampered our playing in the woods behind our house, but it did give us something exciting to watch instead. When we heard the planes coming, we kids all gathered around in our yards or on the curbs along with some adults who happened to be at home (mostly our mamas) and cheered on those pilots' efforts. At that close range it was possible to actually see the pilots very clearly and it became our practice to wave frantically to them as they dove down to land. What a thrill sometimes when they waved back! They were our heroes and we made sure they knew it.

That landing and takeoff practice lasted quite a few weeks during the daytime hours that summer and helped make the war real to us. It became a normal event until one fateful day. One of the pilots who was undoubtedly new at the project veered off course for some reason when he swooped down on our neighborhood attempting to land. He was just off to one side of the field and didn't land, but quickly jerked the nose of the plane upward and managed to miss the house next door to ours, which was looming in his path. He missed crashing into the house, but not altogether. As he pulled the plane sharply upward and a bit sideways the tail dragged behind just enough to bump the chimney of our neighbor's house, taking with it a few bricks. Several other bricks flew into the air and came down randomly like hail. We kids, who were watching as usual, didn't know whether to cheer or run for our lives! Of course a quick getaway was our wise choice and nobody was injured, thank goodness.

That day was the last we saw of those planes and their practicing pilots. They found another field somewhere after having our neighbor's chimney reconstructed. So it was back to running across that field and playing in the woods again for us. Such were the fortunes of war in our little neighborhood.

But that is not the end of the story about planes. Turn to the next chapter to continue.

Watching planes take off and land at Love Field airport.
A favorite pastime that cost nothing.

Planes Falling from the Sky

Not only was our day-to-day safety in a bit of jeopardy with the bi-plane trainers swooping down from the sky and toppling chimneys, but we were also subjected to witness a plane crash disaster nearby our neighborhood.

At the small airfield where the small bi-planes were hangered, sometimes other military aircraft landed there. I imagine it was also for some sort of training purposes or maybe for servicing the planes or maybe taking on fuel. No jet aircraft back then to make long flights without refueling again on the way, and no longer runways needed for the aircraft of that time. However, I never found out where that plane came from or why it was headed for that airfield.

During WWII planes were given names. This plane was named the "Suzy Q." It was a bomber and apparently had a full crew on board. We kids were used to seeing large military planes flying overhead, bound for the various war areas, so we continued playing. We didn't give much thought to this bomber flying over our neighborhood until the motor began to cough and sputter and then the large plane began to nose down sharply while headed away from our neighborhood. We all stopped playing in the street and just froze and watched in horror, because we knew this certainly was not normal. The plane went down a couple of miles away from our street into the area of the small airfield. It was making a lot of noise and other people were standing outside watching in silence with us. We lost sight of it behind the trees and then we heard the awful explosion of the crash and saw the smoke billowing up from it. No one knew what to do. What could we do? What a frightening event for a child to witness. We knew they were all dead. We all just gasped and stood there. We had become accustomed to the newsreels in the theaters showing shots of the war, but this was right here, close to our homes!

Of course we knew not to try to go to the site, and just stayed out of the way at home. So, without TV and with slow radio reporting of local news, we had to wait quite a while to hear about the crash of the "Suzy Q". They said there were no survivors, but we already knew that from what we had witnessed. I don't think any of us ever got over that picture of what could happen to a plane, especially during wartime. It made us kids think about what was happening in other countries and be thankful that we lived here in the United States where all that smoke and damage was an accident, not the result of an enemy lobbing rockets at us. We kids grew up a little faster that day.

Climbing Activities Around the Neighborhood

C limbing is apparently built into the nature or DNA of children. At least it seemed to be with the three of us on Sharon St. My daddy said he never looked for me on the ground as a kid, when I was big enough to climb up on or into something. He didn't seem to understand that from about age six to age ten, for me, there was something exciting about being above ground. Obviously, my playmates of that era felt the same way. The following are a few adventures we enjoyed while satisfying our climbing urges.

"Climbing and Autographs – Crayons in the Attic"

After the war was over, and the homebuilders began to surface again, our beloved field of hills, horned toads and bird nests was taken over by a flurry of dirt spreading and construction of new homes. No more flying kites in that prime location. No more toad petting. No more cowboys and Indians hiding behind the dirt piles. We weren't even allowed to go to that field during the day that summer while the work was in progress. There was a lot of hammering and banging after the tractors left and the foundations were in place for a whole block of houses. The framing went up and the roofs were put on. Every time we kids came around too close while the home building was going on, we were chased away from the area to safety. Our little horned frogs also vacated the area when their dirt pile abodes were flattened. We kids could only sit on the curb at the corner and watch as our field was transformed into a new section of our neighborhood. We sat and talked about how the houses would look and who would eventually move into them. We were curious about just how many kids our age would appear and how they would fit into our activities. We pledged to each other that we would always remain the driving force behind the kidding around on our street. After all, we were the original kid posse around those parts!

One day, while sitting on the curb eating Popsicles and watching the action, we came up with a brilliant idea to help enhance the beauty of those new dwellings. It involved three things: crayons, the ability to climb, and patience until work on the site was finished for the day. We kids were proficient with the artistic use of crayons, and after years of shinnying up trees and onto garage roofs, climbing wasn't a problem. However, patience was another thing. We decided our best bet was to wait until the weekend when no homebuilders were at work. On the weekend our band of three advanced on those still-under-construction houses as stealthily as we had crept around the little dirt piles hiding from each other. This time, we were hiding from everybody else.

Everything was still wide open in each house, so we had no problem entering the target sites. Once inside each house, we all found a way to scramble up the wooden framework and onto the attic beams. There we sat and reached into our pockets for our crayons. We didn't want anyone to be able to see our drawings from below, so we drew on the top of the beams. We wrote our names on them and drew pictures in various colors beside our names. No bad language – we hadn't matured that far yet. Besides, we were artists, not thugs! We took on each house in turn and left our marks. This took a while and we had to be careful not to fall or be discovered. I'll bet all those folks who moved into the finished houses never guessed that our names are written all over their attic rafters – until now! If anyone reading about this kidding around adventure lives in one of those houses, take a look up there. I doubt those crayon autographs have disappeared even after all these years, and those homeowners might see the names of kids, who, without TV or electronic games to amuse them on a weekend, provided their own entertainment up in the unfinished attic of their house.

"Climbing and the Gas Balloons"

Another climbing pleasure was provided by accessibility to the garage roof of our next-door neighbor. That is where the family of one of our posse of three moved from where they were renting across the street and into their new house next door to us. When our mothers went shopping, kids were sometimes left at home. No problem doing that back then, as I have previously stated. There was usually someone at home in a house nearby during the day anyway. One day, when our mothers got together to go shopping, rolling their carts to the shopping strip grocery and drug stores, we three little mischief-makers immediately got to work on our latest project as soon as they were out of sight.

Our homes had gas heaters and in summer the free standing room heaters were usually disconnected from the gas jets jutting from the wall after the jets were turned off, and the heaters were stored away somewhere until the winter. However, three entrepreneurs were well aware of how to turn the key and allow the gas to slowly flow into and inflate the balloons whose mouths were stretched over the open end of the gas jet. Sometimes these balloons were purchased weeks in advance of the time we knew our mothers would make their trek to the grocery for a couple of hours. Here is how it worked: One kid held the balloon mouth firmly in place over the jet while the second kid slowly turned the key to seep the gas into the balloon and inflate it to just the right size without bursting it. Kid two then quickly shut the gas off. Kid number three was standing by with the piece of cut string held in place closely to loop it and tie it securely to the neck of the inflated balloon as it was eased off of the gas jet. As you can see, it took three participants to accomplish this without allowing gas to escape into the room. We quickly became pros at this project. The loose, dangling string attached to the balloon was then looped around a doorknob to hold the balloon until time to launch it. We usually had at least three or four balloons to send off. Before the gas jet operation, notes were written about various subjects and giving the location of our launching. Sometimes those small notes were even rolled up and inserted into the balloons before gassing them up. Other notes were tied to the dangling end of the string. After all balloons were ready, we each took control of a couple of them and exited the back door and climbed onto the back porch railing and up onto the roof of the garage. The balloon launching ceremony then began. Those colorful little globes floated up and into the air beautifully, one by one while we cheered and clapped them on to greater height! The only disappointing thing about this "scientific" endeavor was that we never did hear from anyone who found one of our little ventures into space. Nobody seemed to care. Actually, the thrill was in the secret inflating and spectacular launching, while not being discovered by our parents. As we grew older, however, we became more aware of the gas jet dangers and discontinued that game. Actually, we outgrew playing with balloons, and there were many more adventures out there in which we could become involved. However, climbing onto the garage roof still remained a favorite pastime.

"Climbing Onto Our Rooftop Clubhouse"

Another "clubhouse" play area was atop the storage-shed addition to the back of the garage of one of the folks living across the street. They had no children and if they knew we climbed on the fence and pulled ourselves up to the roof of their shed, they never complained to our parents or us. We three kids would take snacks up there in our pockets and sit atop the shed roof and talk and laugh and eat and plan our next adventure of kiddom. We called our hideout "The Green Lantern". This was a reference to a place where one of the heroes of our time and his posse hung out. We would sit up there without electronics and use our little brains to imagine things we would do someday to show the world how special we were. And we were special, and so were our parents – together we survived that Great Depression plus a World War and emerged with our sense of humor in tact. Quite an accomplishment for such a dark time in our country, especially for three kids who had to get along with less and still have fun, even if some things we did were admittedly a bit dangerous. But, we were fearless!

"Climbing Up The Sycamore Tree"

Climbing seemed to be something we kids felt compelled to do as often as possible and in as many places as we could. However there was only one tree in the neighborhood large enough to hold us. It was a Sycamore tree and it had been there for a long time evidently. It was in the grassy parkway in front of the house of one of my pals, so it was deemed to belong to all of us. This tall tree was actually the first football-kicking goal we devised. I was the only one of our group that could manage to kick the ball over the top of the tree. Quite a feat for a skinny kid, but a reasonable accomplishment for a tomboy.

We could not reach the lower branches of this tall tree while standing on the ground, so we used my daddy's garage workshop to cut short pieces of boards into slats to use as steps. We nailed them at intervals up the trunk of the tree up to the large lower limb and used them to climb up into the tree. Later we decided that sitting on a limb was not as comfortable as we thought it might be. So, we recruited our daddies to help us get a more comfortable perch. Our dads were really good at woodworking and were proud to be the designers and architects of our new tree house. They cut pieces of plywood to fit the spaces between several large limbs in the tree and nailed them across the limbs so that all three of us could sit and dangle our skinny legs down over the street They attached some slats of wood around the sides to form a railing on three sides, with the side next to the tree left open as an entrance and exit. We had not planned on falling out of the tree, but adding those rails was a parental precaution to preserve the lives of three nutty kids.

Sitting up there on that platform gabbing or eating snacks or just chilling out in the shade of that big old tree, was what we did while waiting for the invention of TV, electronic games and cell phones. But what else was there to do before all those modern inventions happened – besides riding bikes, that is. Actually, we did discover another way of amusing ourselves, right up there in that old tree.

Sycamore trees have small, golf-ball-size balls hanging down from the limbs. We used to pick them off and throw them down into the street. When they hit the ground, they released feathery spore plumes. We would watch as those fluffy things scattered and blew into the air when they hit. That scene developed another idea for a bit of kidding around for us. In those days there were not many cars driving up and down our streets. No cars were parked at the curbs in front of our houses, primarily because there was usually only one family car – if they had one – and it was parked either in the driveway or in the garage. So, as we sat on our perch up in the Sycamore tree an idea eventually hatched. Wouldn't it be fun to pick a few Sycamore balls and "lay in wait" until a car passed by below our tree, and then drop the furry balls to explode atop the passing cars? So we did. It was fun until we got caught! Drivers were really surprised when a barrage of thumps happened overhead, and their windshields were full of feathery stuff. Most of them slowed down and then drove away when they saw it wasn't something to hurt them or their vehicle. Some drivers got out of the car and scanned the neighborhood for the cause of the thumps. After looking around and seeing no one who looked like a fuzzy ball-throwing criminal, they would get back into their cars and drive away. They didn't know where it came from and never looked up into the tree to catch the culprits. We never thought that it could cause an accident! We were lucky that didn't occur. Our parents discovered what we were doing and put a stop to it before something happened that we would regret later. It's a good thing parents are smarter than kids. We still threw Sycamore balls down into the street to watch them burst – just not at cars or people anymore. We weren't trying to be bad – just amusing ourselves kidding around.

Climbing wasn't the only thing we did for fun around the neighborhood. There were other adventures lurking all around us just waiting for us to discover them. Following is one that didn't require climbing, but did involve a tree.

"The Old Pear Tree"

This tree was not one that we were allowed to climb. It grew in the back yard of the house across the street, where a couple lived who had no children at home. They seldom came outside, but seemed to enjoy the three of us who lived across from and next door to them. Their pear tree was really large and shaded most of their backyard. This nice couple gave us permission to eat a pear from their tree now and then. Actually there were so many pears that there were a lot of them rotting on the ground before they could be picked. They even put some baskets under the tree to catch them. But we kids just rode our bikes down their driveway and into their yard, leaned the bikes against the trunk of the tree, stood up on the bike seat and helped ourselves to a nice big pear picked fresh from a lower hanging limb. This fruity treat, picked fresh from the tree at no cost to us, was really priceless in those days when we were recovering from the depression and fresh fruit was pretty pricey. Those pears were one of the things we feasted on up on our "Green Lantern" clubhouse over those generous people's storage shed. They knew we picked the pears – they didn't know where we went to eat them while discussing the next escapade we were contemplating.

Pomegranates On The Roof

When the Sharon St. posse felt the urge to roam from our own street, but still not out of the neighborhood, we sometimes walked (yes, we walked a lot in those days) over one block to a house in the middle of the block where a Pomegranate tree grew in the back yard. The folks who lived there had no children and were very nice to the three of us when we showed up. They knew why we were visiting them, and allowed us to pick some of the fruit from their tree, since it produced a large crop of pomegranates. Like the folks with the pear tree, there was more than enough fruit for them to eat, so they were glad to share.

On these treks, we carried small bags and loaded them with the fruit and then did something the residents there didn't see us do. We took our sacks of fruit and climbed onto the board fence next to their detached garage. From there we managed to pull ourselves up onto the low hanging garage roof. Since we were all adept at climbing, this was not as dangerous as it sounds. We would then crawl up near the top of the roof on the side of the garage facing away from their house. Don't ask me why, but this is where we chose to eat those delicious, tart pomegranate seeds.

For those not familiar with pomegranates, they are about the size of an orange and when you break open the fruit, it is filled with pretty reddish-pink seeds, which are coated with the juicy part of the fruit. You pluck the seeds out one at a time and suck the juice and minimal pulp from the small seeds. After that, you spit out the still pink seed and start on the next one. Needless to say, it took a while to eat the many seeds from even one pomegranate! But time was all that we had in the summer, so we didn't mind. We just sat up there, out of sight, sucking on the tart, fruity seeds and spitting them out while we planned our next adventure. Where did we spit them? All over part of the garage roof, of course. This probably doesn't sound like a big problem, and actually it wasn't. Except that the seeds were pink and faded onto anything they touched, including our mouths, fingers, and that side of the garage roof. We only spit them in one area, because they made the roof slick and we needed an exit route that wasn't dangerous. However, they covered a large area of the roof.

Somehow that seemed to be a pretty sight to us – a roof turning pink in a large spot. Kind of a dirty trick, however, played on the generous folks who shared their fruit with us. But it was not on the side of the garage roof that they could see from their house or yard, and it pretty well washed off when it rained anyway. Probably not the nicest way we could repay them, but, hey, they had the most colorful pink garage roof (on one side) on their street! Maybe if they had noticed the pink on their garage, they would have had second thoughts about having their own children or sharing with other folk's kids. But we really didn't permanently damage anything, and as usual, we were just kids – amusing ourselves. Nothing wrong with that! Anyway, we thought that pinkish garage roof was pretty cool.

Picking Up Pecans and Persimmons

In the fall, and usually on Sunday afternoons, my daddy would pack us all into our little Ford car and drive out to the country to hunt pecan trees out in the woods. Besides my daddy and me, the other passengers on these trips were my mama, my aunt and my grandmother. My daddy drove, with my mama sitting up front with him and the rest of us crammed into the back seat of the car, with me in the middle. With no heat or air conditioning in the cars then, I didn't much mind being closely positioned like that when the weather was chilly. I was actually pretty warm with a long sleeved shirt, heavy sweater, corduroy pants, long socks, boots and a toboggan hat on my head. All those clothes felt pretty good out in the woods for an hour on foot cruising around looking on the ground for all the pecans I could drop into my paper bag. We must have looked like squirrels foraging for food, as we moved around bent over looking for the good pecans. When some big good ones were spotted still clinging to the tree branches, my daddy would find a large stick and either reach up and knock them off or throw the stick at them to make them fall. He even wrapped his arms around the tree sometimes and shook the tree to make the nuts fall. When he did all of these actions, it was time to retreat out of the way to avoid getting popped on the head with a pecan or a falling stick. We had the routine perfectly timed.

My aunt usually brought a nutcracker and little picks with us so that we could sample some of our bounty right out there in the woods. After the hunt, when our bags were amply loaded, we usually sat down and cracked a few pecans, trying to successfully pick out a whole half. There was a certain amount of skill involved doing that. We all tried to crack them just so, and shell them out just right so that a complete half nut would pop out of the shell and not be broken into pieces. There was definitely an art to producing a perfect half nut. Most people probably know what a hand-held cracker is and maybe they even have used one, but the little pick used after the nut is cracked is the instrument one must wield artistically to

190

achieve the release of a whole half from the shell. Not many shelling artists achieve that. When a whole half was achieved, it was placed in a separate bag to be used for pies and other goodies, but we ate some of the broken ones right then. I was never too accomplished at producing a perfect half, sometimes deliberately, so I got to eat a lot of imperfect pieces as a reward for my diligent nut gathering. We sat on our front porch later and finished shelling. The shells were then scattered around the flowerbeds to recycle them and help the soil. That's what I was told, at least. We didn't waste much back then.

The pecan hunts were not just something we did for fun. Those delicious native discoveries were always soon put to good use in pies and other goodies at Thanksgiving and Christmas. These days, people just don't know what they are missing when they purchase their packages of already shelled pecans at great prices. The hunt was part of the fun. The real objective was to produce the yummy treats we enjoyed together later.

For another good foraging experience, we always dropped by one of the golf courses that had a very prolific persimmon tree at the edge of the course next to the roadway. You must be careful when seeking persimmons, since some of those that have fallen to the ground under the tree are really mushy and nasty. That's not something you want to step on! The persimmons still on the tree can sometimes not be ripe enough to pick and consume; therefore, we only took only a few home each time when we located the ripe ones. My aunt and grandmother seemed to have the knack for knowing which ones were ripe enough to eat. But if you tried to eat a persimmon that was still not ripe, your mouth would pucker so bad that you might not want to try another one! Those ripe ones were sure good and a very unusual treat. I don't know how we discovered the tree, because it seemed to be the only one in the whole area where we lived. Nobody could figure out why it was growing there on the edge of the golf course. I really enjoyed eating the pecans much more than the persimmons, but my grandmother liked that odd fruit, and that was all that mattered at the time.

There is something missing in today's world in a lot of communities, I believe. It is called family togetherness and respect. It's not all about the fruit – it's really all about the folks.

Pecan Foraging

Sometimes it was cold and sometimes we hunted pecans
in our short sleeves.

There was no real dress code for that activity.
However, my mama insisted that my ears were covered by
a scarf or hat in the Fall.

Earaches were not something she wanted to deal with.

The Great Escape - - - A Close Call!

T he father of one of my neighborhood pals on Sharon Street was a U. S. Marshall. In later years, he took his family back to his hometown in another city in Texas, where he successfully ran for sheriff several times, serving for many years.

When he was our neighbor, he and my daddy became good friends. Since my daddy's hobby was photography, and he frequently made photos of things happening around the neighborhood, all of our neighbors were aware of his photography obsession. He was always taking pictures of we neighborhood kids in action. He even made a movie, which he also scripted, of a fictional happening involving our neighbors. You will read about that movie in a subsequent chapter. One of my greatest regrets is that most of those old photos and the movie have been lost in various moves to other residential locations. However, the best movie and still photos he made were on a "business" trip with our neighbor.

One summer, my daddy and our U.S. Marshall neighbor began discussing the fact that the Marshall sometimes was responsible for transporting local prisoners to a penitentiary elsewhere in the United States. This neighbor was a no-nonsense individual, but very nice and extremely likeable. He was no "Matt Dillon", but came pretty close to that image. He doted on his only child, who was adopted, and who was one of my closest neighborhood buddies. Several times, this family hosted our little one-child family at their farm, which was located outside of the town where the man would eventually become sheriff. On those visits to their farm, he taught his son and me to fire several weapons at a target, while he impressed upon us the need for extreme safety precautions with firearms. I still have that healthy respect for them to this day! My daddy watched closely while this instruction was happening, but my mama always retreated to the house when the guns came out. She also had respect for them and wanted to be well out of the line of fire, I suspect. However, we never had a problem with them and learned to be pretty accurate with firearms on those visits.

Now back to the discussion between our dads, on one of those farm visits, regarding prisoner transporting. Of course, as my pal and I were learning to shoot guns, my daddy was clicking away with his camera. That is when the Marshall came up with the brilliant idea of taking my daddy along on one of those trips, carrying both his movie and still cameras, to make a documentary of the transporting of prisoners starting at the local jail all the way to a penitentiary. The Marshall's next prisoner transporting trip was to be in a few weeks to the prison in Leavenworth, Kansas. The two dads decided it would be a good idea, and that they would discuss it with the heads of the Marshall's office to see if they could obtain clearance to do that recording of prisoner transport. They met with the people who would make that decision and received permission and support from them to proceed with their idea in the form of a documentary. The prisoner to be moved was not a dangerous person, so no other law enforcement officer was needed in the transfer. However, they required that my daddy be deputized, and he was given specific instructions about his role in the venture. I imagine my daddy's reputation with the "Y" and his occasional strength building classes for members of the police department was a subject that came up in the discussion and was a plus in the decision to let him ride with the Marshall. The agreement also included paying all my daddy's expenses, including the film, plus $200 for making the documentary. That was a lot of money back in those days, so there was no argument with that aspect of the deal. In addition, they required that all still photos and movie film shot would become the property of the U. S. Marshall's office for the purpose of documentation and training purposes. My daddy would have liked to have had a copy of all his photographic work, but that was the deal they made, and all the film he shot was turned over to the Marshall's office as soon as they returned. Little did they all know how important his work would eventually prove to be. As you can imagine, my mama was a bit apprehensive and not in favor of this project, but my daddy assured her the prisoner was harmless, so she relented and gave up the argument. She convinced herself that it was a good photographic opportunity for my daddy and opportunities like that didn't come along everyday.

A couple of weeks later, my daddy took a few days vacation and joined the Marshall and his prisoner for the trip to Leavenworth prison. They left very early in the morning in a Marshall's office car, with my daddy in the front passenger seat and the prisoner in the back seat in handcuffs. After a few hours of driving, they stopped for lunch at a roadside diner on the way to the prison. One of the prisoner's hands was released from the handcuffs so that he could feed himself. All went well during their meal. After lunch, the prisoner asked to use the restroom before returning to the car. He would be allowed to be in there alone while my daddy and the Marshall waited outside, standing guard at the door. No other persons would be allowed in the restroom while he was in there. Then he would be escorted back to the car and the handcuffs would be placed on both hands and the Marshall and my daddy would alternate watching him while the other used the restroom in the diner. After the prisoner was escorted to the restroom and my daddy and the Marshall stood watch at the door, the Marshall began to get an uneasy feeling that the prisoner had been in the restroom too long. Must have been either a gut feeling or past experience that made him check on the prisoner. When he opened the door and went to the booths, he discovered that the prisoner was no longer in the restroom. When he looked into the booth at the far end of the room, he was met with the sight of an open window. The Marshall immediately charged out of the restroom toward the front door of the diner and yelled at my daddy to follow him. My daddy had brought his movie camera into the diner with them, and as he ran to catch up to the Marshall, he began shooting the action of the Marshall sprinting to the front door. They ran around the side of the diner and spotted the prisoner behind the diner inching his way down a sloping grassy area. When he reached the bottom of the slope, he began to run across an open field. The Marshall was already sliding down the slope and starting to run after him. My daddy stood on the high ground and continued to film the action in front of him. As the Marshall began gaining on the prisoner, he yelled at him to stop or he would be shot. The prisoner continued to run. He may not have been dangerous, but he sure enough didn't want to go to prison! My daddy continued to grind away with his camera. Since the prisoner refused to stop, the Marshall took aim and shot him in the ankle just above his heel. At that point, the prisoner dropped to the ground and the chase was over. Everything stopped except my daddy's finger on the movie camera button! He continued shooting film when the medics came. The wound was not critical – just enough to disable the man and prevent him from further flight. After he was patched up, the journey continued to the prison. What a crack shot that Marshall was, being able to wound a guy just enough to bring him down but not interrupt the trip to the prison for several days. On the other hand, it seems a bit negligent not to have been outside the window of the restroom to prevent the whole episode in the first place. Or so it seems to me. Anyway, it made for a great documentary. Needless to say, the Marshall's office got a lot more than they bargained for, and my daddy had an exciting photo opportunity.

When the two dads returned home and told us about the exciting trip, I asked my daddy if he was scared. He said he was too busy filming to be scared at the time, but that it hit him later. He said he was glad the prisoner was not a violent person and was just trying to avoid prison. He said all that in front of my mama. She put her tiny size 4 foot down to further discussion of doing that again. Later, when we were alone, I asked my daddy again if he wasn't just a little bit scared. He just said, "What do you think?" I thought I would not have been a little bit scared...I would have been a whole lot scared.

Miss Butch

One day when we three kids were sitting there on a rock by the stream eating our lunch in the park about a mile from our neighborhood, a stray medium sized black dog joined us for lunch. There were no leash laws in those days, so there were a lot of dogs running around out there. After feasting on our sandwiches, we decided to share what was left with the dog. Nobody ever ate the crusts of their bread, so there was quite a lot left over. The dog quickly devoured the leftover scraps and began thanking us by licking us. This was a really nice friendly dog, we thought. So, we decided that if the dog came home with us we would ask if one of us could keep it. After that meal and attention we paid it, of course it followed us home. After we jumped back on our bikes and headed home, the dog trotted along behind us. It probably had no home, so we didn't discourage it from following us. When we arrived back in the neighborhood, we introduced our parents to the dog and asked if one of us could keep it as a pet. None of us had a pet. We told them of our plans to actually share the responsibility of the dog's care. The parents of one of the boys finally relented and allowed him to keep the mongrel dog, provided we three kept our promise to look after its care. It never occurred to any of us to examine the dog to determine the sex. We had already collaborated to name the dog "Butch". When we told the parents what we had decided to name the dog, they just laughed. Why? Because that dog was a female and the name didn't exactly fit. So we expanded on it and renamed her "Miss Butch". We three amigos agreed it was going to be a joint effort to properly feed and groom her and teach her to do tricks. That endeavor surprisingly went pretty smoothly and quickly. The dog loved the attention and blossomed before our eyes. They say a mixed breed or mongrel dog is smarter than a pure breed, and I can believe that theory, because we were successful in just about everything we tried to teach Miss Butch. The absence of a leash law allowed her to roam freely at will and with the three of us everywhere we went. But that's not the end of the Miss Butch story.

Since my daddy had such an avid love of photography as a hobby, he took many photos of the three of us romping around with Miss Butch and teaching her tricks. What a neat and smart pet she turned out to be. She learned quickly and was so friendly that everyone loved her. After watching us become so attached to her, my daddy came up with the brilliant idea of making a home movie with the dog as the main character. Here is the plot my daddy came up with: While he was filming everything that happened, we kids would act out the script he gave us. We would all ride our bikes back to the park and "find" a dog, feed it lunch and bring it home – just as it really happened. The next Saturday afternoon as we rode our bikes, the daddy of the dog's new owner slowly drove his car behind us, with my daddy hanging his movie camera out of the window, following us to and from the park. Miss Butch was riding with them in the car, sitting in the back seat as though she was doing something she had always done. We even took sandwiches and fed the dog the scraps while my daddy was whirring away with his camera. We had to make a lot of gestures depicting what was happening, because this was, after all, a silent home movie. We were pretty good little actors. That's what kids do all the time – play around and make believe. As we all left the park, we kids riding our bikes with the dog trailing after us as before, my daddy and our neighbor drove behind us still filming the caravan from the car window. That smart animal was a natural. She put Lassie in the shade as far as acting is concerned! She seemed to know exactly what was going on.

The photo shoot continued at home with the other parents entering the picture and giving the O.K. to keeping the dog and our promising to care for her. Let me say at this point that my daddy used plain white paper to make quoted titles describing the action and then he included them in the movie before and after the moving shots. It looked much like the way they did it in the old silent movies. These were very clear as to what was going on in the movie. After this had all taken place, my daddy then revealed to all of us the rest of the plot. He would dress up like a tramp in old dirty clothes and one of the neighbors would act as the cameraman while my daddy did his part of the acting. This involved him sneaking down the alley and attempting to steal the dog. In those days, alleys in our neighborhoods were not paved and until somebody had time to mow behind their house, the grass and weeds were usually pretty overgrown.

This made the sneaky tramp look even more sinister as he slipped down the alley giving furtive glances around as he peered into the backyards looking for something to steal. All this time our neighbor was following him with the camera and also with some of the other neighbors trailing behind the cameraman watching the action. Of course, our gang of three was right there, also. Let me describe the attire of my daddy the tramp: He had on an old dirty felt hat pulled low over his brow, a dirty shirt and a pair of baggy pants tied at the waist with a rope instead of a belt. I don't know where on earth they came up with all that costume. I never saw any of it around our house! Of course, we had all practiced this part of the movie, and the dog just seemed instinctively to know exactly what we wanted her to do. (Look out Lassie!) She just went right along with whatever we urged her to do.

The yard where our new dog lived was behind a wooden fence with a wooden gate opening into the alley. In our movie, this gate was left open just a bit and Miss Butch was tied up close to the fence. This was something new for her because she had already adopted us all and had no idea of leaving. She knew what side of her bread the butter was on and who put it there! She was home. She didn't need to be tied. My daddy had previously worked with the dog being tied up and had somehow taught her to resist and hold back and refuse to follow when he tried to tug the rope and drag her away. She was a real trooper and went along with the plan, with all of us cheering her on to refuse to follow him. She had never growled at any of us, so the growling part had to be included in the movie's titles describing the action. My daddy would tug the rope, the dog would pull back, and the growling title would appear on the screen. That is how it went as my daddy "the tramp" attempted to kidnap the dog, get out the gate and sneak off back down the alley. (The only problem with this scenario was that we had never had a tramp in our alleys or anywhere else around our houses. It was all my daddy's imagination going wild.)

The next scene showed we three pals calling the dog and looking all over the neighborhood with my daddy running along behind us with the camera. When we couldn't find her, he filmed us running to our parents for help. There was lots of crying and emoting by the three budding kid actors. (More titles) The next scene was of three sad kids sitting on the porch steps, lined up like birds on a wire, with our elbows on our knees and our chins cupped in our hands giving serious thought to finding our dog. At this point the dog, according to the titles, had been gone for several days. It actually did take several days and weekends to get all this action on film.

Next scene: My daddy in his tramp outfit sitting by a small fire on a rock beside the creek in the park cooking a hot dog over the fire, speared on a small stick. A few feet away was Miss Butch tied to a small tree behind him. We smeared some dog food on the rope and we urged her to gnaw on it. We had to continue smearing it on the rope until she apparently got the idea and kept chewing until she chewed through it. While the tramp sat with his back to the dog, concentrating on his cooking, Miss Butch gnawed through the rope and silently escaped. Again the other daddy was the cameraman. After the rope was chewed through, there was a couple of feet of it still around the dog's neck. We three pals were the audience this time. The dog had been brought back to the park in the car, but when we all left she was put on the ground behind the car and we all rode in the car calling to her and urging her to follow the car as we drove home. She had no intention of letting us get away from her after all that had been going on with the movies and the petting and the car trips. She gained momentum as the car took off and ran at top speed behind us while my daddy (still in his tramp costume) filmed her out the window – backward this time. But after a couple of blocks of running and filming, we put her back into the car where she rode in style the rest of the way home, with us petting her and telling her what a good job she did. She already knew it! That was one smart dog. As soon as we arrived back home we set up another scene while my daddy acted as the cameraman. We took our places back on the front porch in our sad posturing. (Look out Our Gang!) As we suddenly looked up (title here of a bark) and saw Miss Butch running up to us, we all fell upon her and hugged her while my daddy circled around the heap of us on the ground grinding away on his camera. The final title read, "Miss Butch was safely back home." What a fun summer that was. Three free-to-roam kids, a new dog, and aspiring movie stars. Couldn't get much better than that! But, wait…

After my daddy developed the film (he did his own processing, splicing, editing and printing), we had a "premier" party at our house complete with refreshments. An event that caused my mama to open up the living room. All the neighbors came and agreed we were good actors – especially Miss Butch. Can you imagine a neighborhood today getting together on a project such as this? I hate to invoke "the good old days" here, but they really were, in spite of what was going on in our country and around the world. We found a way to keep us all pulling together in simple, fun ways. Times were bad, but we were all good – good at working together and having simple fun. It really was "the good old days", and we were special!

But that is still not the end of the story – there is more and it was added to the film later. This occurred after summer was about over and we were about to go back to school.

Apparently there was a Mister Butch somewhere around the neighborhood that we didn't know about and never did. Our Miss Butch delivered five cute, chubby, wiggly puppies. She was a great mother and how could our film have ended more perfectly. But as these pups were getting old enough to be weaned, something very bad happened to me while we were just kidding around. You will find out about it next. Read on…

The Broken Hip

One summer, between sixth and seventh grade, the daddy of one of my neighborhood buddies decided to build a second story above their detached garage, to be used as a playroom for us kids. This proved to be a great play place for us to kid around. It had lots of storage and a ping-pong table and a pool table. It also had a small table on which we could play board games. Since there was no air conditioning in those days, we used windows and fans up there to keep us cool. We didn't seem to mind the heat like kids do today in air-conditioned environments. This was also a nice place to play in winter, out of the rain and cold. No heat except a small heater, but we all had jackets anyway.

Eventually that wonderful playroom would turn out to be my downfall. As kids will often do, we found another use for that upstairs getaway that would begin another chapter in my life.

One afternoon, we three kids were bored with playing pool, ping-pong, and board games, and came up with another activity involving the playroom. It was wartime, so we decided to play a war game. With no electronic games in those days, we had to make up our own war games. This particular game, which we had not played before, involved old bed sheets. We all went to our houses and sneaked out an old sheet from the dirty clothes hamper. It was necessary to sneak them out, because we knew in our hearts that our mamas would never allow one of their sheets to be drug out and manhandled by three crazy kids. So what would we use the sheets for in a war game? Jumping out of the upstairs playroom window, using the sheets as parachutes, of course. Only the three of us could have come up with this plan to amuse ourselves on a summer day. Naturally, we all recognized this as not a very good idea, which explains our furtive pick up and transport of the sheets to the playroom.

The plan was to fold the sheet, then hold the four corners, two in each hand, to form a parachute. Crude engineering, but that didn't occur to our little almost ten year old kidding around minds. We just needed to end the boredom. After getting the sheets gathered in hand, we planned to sit on the upstairs playroom windowsill and scooted off the ledge, holding the sheet over our heads to catch the air and float us to the ground and break the impact of the landing. Bad decision and bad engineering plan! The two boys, who were both barefoot, went first and landed pretty well without getting hurt – amazingly! Then it was my turn. I was barefoot also, but before I jumped I slipped into my shoes, thinking it would hurt my bare feet when I landed. I did exactly as planned, but apparently my chute was too large and it did not unfold and open up enough to catch the wind as it was supposed to do. Instead I landed on the ground flat on both feet. Plop! Like a rock! It hurt for a few minutes, but I continued to play in the yard on the swing set. We had all decided that one jump was enough, and in my case, it was more then enough. Later we secreted our folded up sheets back to our homes and replaced them where we had found them. No one was the wiser. That is, until a few days later when I began to have pain in my hip and leg and began to walk with a limp, which was quickly observed by my mama. She began to question me about our activities so that she could pinpoint the problem. The story of the parachute episode finally surfaced and I was quickly taken to the doctor's office for x-rays of my hip.

The x-rays confirmed the fracture to my right hip. I was so scared! Nobody in our neighborhood had ever had a broken bone. I didn't know what to expect. The wheels began to turn quickly and I was carried home and put to bed on my tummy. No cast, no surgery. Just told to lay quietly in bed on my stomach. In those days, the process of surgically pinning hips had not yet been thought of – thank goodness! Because of the location of the break, they tell me if it had been pinned, I probably would have walked with a stiff leg limp. I found out much later that the doctor wasn't even sure it would heal or knit back together, because of how it looked on the x-ray and where the break occurred. He told my parents that it had only a 50-50 chance of healing properly. Of course, this information was not passed along to me at the time.

So, I endured laying flat on my stomach with my leg perfectly still to see if the crack in the hip joint would knit back together. Maybe the word "endure" is not the proper word here. I was totally miserable! Can you imagine how hard it was for an overactive kid to lay still on her stomach 24 hours a day for eight weeks? Don't try this at home – you won't like it! I was missing out on all the kidding around going on in the neighborhood, even though my two buddies did visit me and read comic books and talk to me and encourage me to lay still and heal. Not even a TV set to entertain me. My daddy devised a carrier board to slip under me; so that each morning before he went to work he could transport me to my parents' bed to spend the day, because it was closer to the kitchen and living area of our house. This also helped my mama keep a closer eye on me. Good thing I was a skinny beanpole of a kid, making it easier to move me from room to room on my "magic carpet board". Eating was not so pleasant either, propped on my elbows for a short time while on my stomach. The only time I was on my back was when I needed to use the bedpan. Bed baths required a bit of adjusting, also, but my mama managed to handle that task nicely. The point of the whole ordeal for everyone was to not bend the hip or move it around – just keep it still and straight. I think a cast would have been much easier to handle, but the location of the crack was not in a place where a cast could be used.

And you should have seen how my hair was cleaned! Some sort of granules was used as I hung my head off of the bed over a newspaper. They were rubbed into the hair and scalp to remove the oil and dirt. Then the hair was brushed well, over the paper, to remove the gritty granules. Somehow it worked – at least for the eight weeks I was assigned to a bed. My hair grew longer and one of our neighbors who knew how to French braid hair would come to our house every few days to braid my growing locks. This wonderful lady also played the piano. The piano was still located in my parents' bedroom, so while I was confined to the bed in that room daily, this wonderful neighbor came to our house everyday and played and sang for me. She could play anything without a sheet of music! She played "Kitten On The Keys" better than anyone I have ever heard! I would request songs and she played and we all sang them. This was not an easy task, either, lying on my stomach. Sometimes that kind neighbor lady brought her husband with her on the weekends when he was not at work. He played the banjo while she played the piano and they both sang just about every song popular in those days. What wonderful folks they were. I think it is unfortunate that we don't see that much neighborly love anymore. I stayed in touch with these folks for many years, even into my adulthood. Their acts of love still overwhelm me.

As will sometimes happen, something they called tuberculosis of the bone can occur. Now, all you doctors don't have a hissy if this is not the case. That is what I remember them telling me, true or not. At any rate, a visiting nurse came by and administered a tuberculosis test on my arm. It was supposed to redden and swell if it was a "positive" test. Mine did. Nobody was happy about that, of course, but I still remained on my tummy for the required eight weeks before any other x-rays were done. Fortunately for me, the test turned out to be a false positive. There is something in my anatomy that will always give a false reading from one of those tests. Phew!

I was also going to miss about four weeks of seventh grade when school began again the next month. I was one of those kids that actually loved school. But everyone spoiled me badly, and that was the only thing that carried me through this ordeal. My schoolteachers even brought my lessons and homework to our house, so that I could keep up with my school grade. My mama helped me with lessons and homework and my teachers even came to the house to give me tests. They were verbal, since it was pretty hard to write laying flat on my stomach, almost as hard as it was to eat in that position. Everyone was so positive with their actions, even though there was still the possibility that the hip would not knit back. Of course, at that time, I didn't know that part, so I just accepted the spoiling by everyone involved. Actually, can you imagine a teacher these days taking the time to do what those teachers back then did for a child – and on their own time! Bless every one of them! They knew none of that was easy for me being flat on my stomach, and they rose to the occasion.

During the time of my confinement, "Miss Butch", our neighborhood mongrel pet, had a litter of puppies. We never discovered the identity of the daddy, but they were cute little pups. Of course, I couldn't get outside to see them, so they were brought to our house in a box to visit me. After I fell in love with the smallest puppy, which they called the runt of the bunch, my parents finally allowed me to adopt the doggie. The cute little ball of fur slept with me and played all around me on the bed. He was not black as his mother was. He was a sort of blonde color. I named him "Nappy" because of his rather bushy appearance. Since it was necessary for him to go outside to take care of business, he was in and out of the house frequently. He also occasionally crossed the street to visit his family. Dogs were allowed to roam the street in those days, unfortunately. It was unfortunate for Nappy, because one late afternoon as he was crossing the street, he ran in front of a car and was hit. My daddy grabbed him up and put him in our car and rushed him to a vet. However, Nappy was so badly injured that he couldn't survive his accident. I was devastated! I cried for days.

My mama and daddy were constantly comforting me anyway, and they really stepped it up after the loss of my little puppy. Even though they were constantly trying to be upbeat and cheerful and positive, one thing I remember happening was people visiting while I was confined to bed and doing a lot of praying. Nobody is going to argue with that activity, but it did make me rather uneasy.

Then came the day for a return trip to the bone doctor. The eight weeks of tummy position was about to end and the doctor wanted to take another look at the fracture. So my daddy carried me to the car on my board and I lay on the back seat during the ride to the doctor's office. When we arrived there, he carried me into the building laying flat on my board. That must have been quite a struggle for him, even though he was a physically very fit man. And I imagine it must have looked petty unique to those who observed him carrying me on that board!

More x-rays were taken. My mama and daddy and I waited in the exam room for the results. Suddenly the door burst open and the doctor came into the room, very excited, waving the x-ray and saying that a miracle had happened! The bone had completely knitted back into the proper place. I wasn't a dummy, and that is when I finally realized that there was a huge doubt that the fractured hip would heal. Probably all those sincere prayers had been better than a pin or a cast. Ya think? I do! Needless to say, there were tears of joy all around. The scripture quotes "Prayer changes things" as well as "God moves in mysterious ways His wonders to perform" are two scriptures with which I must totally agree! I still believe that with all my heart. And I can't tell you how much I learned in eight weeks about the concern and caring of my mama and daddy and many friends and neighbors and teachers. God's mercy and healing and the concern of those folks brought a miracle to a kid in distress. I can't say "Thank You" enough!

So, once again, after much lecturing from the doctor about being more careful, I was going to be an active kid going back to school and just kidding around the neighborhood.

Not very long after that experience in my life, I began to understand what our preacher was trying to convey to us, as well as how those prayers had benefited me. So, I gave my little heart to Jesus and became a Christian. Best decision I ever made. No kidding!

Twelve

When I was twelve years old, my beloved mama passed away.

Time to grow up now.

It wasn't easy, but somehow, with the help of
God and my family and friends,
I managed to do it.

No more kidding around, but oh, what wonderful memories of being a
"Depression Baby . . . Just Kidding Around".

Afterword

I realize that this book ended on a rather somber note. However, in the beginning I said that it was about growing up just kidding around during the Great Depression, and about the time of the ending of my story, the depression had also ended and my life was about to change drastically.

I could write another book – or maybe two -continuing my life's story with chapters on dating, learning to dance, living with my aunt, getting married, raising a Down Syndrome son and a beautiful daughter who thought horses were what life was all about, and how we ultimately built a house in the country with a barn that cost more than our first two houses – just to shelter her 6 horses and several dogs. It taught her to value life, because she was responsible for their care. It kept all of us pretty busy! She now takes care of me as if I am one of her children. Funny how things evolve in life. I guess it is true that what goes around comes around.

I could also write a book about being one of five people who began a sheltered workshop for my son and others with retardation back in 1971. The program grew from a $6,000 investment in a rented space, originally serving only 5 challenged young adults, into a million dollar plus non-profit business, which is still operating and now provides sheltered employment and training for several hundred challenged individuals in three buildings that the corporation owns and two other rented locations. This program gave my son's simple life real meaning. He wanted to go to work everyday. It gave him a feeling of accomplishment that nothing else ever did. I consider my involvement in this endeavor my own 15 minutes of fame. I still sit on the board of directors of the corporation. A former boss of mine told me I should write a book about helping get this program started and funded. I think I will let the program speak for itself, since it has grown and become so successful over the past 40 years. This success came with the guidance and experience and caring of a couple of people who need to write their own book about their journey into improving the lives of mentally and physically challenged adults.

I could include in another book the pain of losing my husband of 35 years to a heart attack when I was only in my mid fifties. I could write about the problems of growing older and surviving breast cancer in my 70s. I could write an entire book about the joy of having grandchildren whom I adore, but I am waiting until they become famous so I can write about them. Or maybe I could even write a book about some of the nuts I have known. Goodness knows there were many over the years. Many of my friends have also told me that I should write a book. They never pinpointed the subject, however.

But there you have those books in a condensed nutshell version. It wouldn't be as much fun to write about struggling through and surviving adult life, as it was to write this account of growing up a happy kid in a not so happy time. So let's just leave well enough alone.

As the old monk once said: "The book is written. Now let the writer play"